Praise for

LAWRENCE OSBORNE'S

PARIS DREAMBOOK

"For the *truly* adventurous traveler, [this is] an unorthodox guide to Paris's down-at-the-heels charms and insidious attractions. Not for Osborne are the City of Light's tourist haunts...for fantasy is [his] stock in trade, [and] he can always locate what he wants..."
—*Booklist*

"[A] hyperbolic ode to the City of Light...Osborne's writing flows like the opaque waters of the Seine."
—Ginger Danto, *Entertainment Weekly*

"Unusual...in dream-like essays, [Osborne] offers his impressions of...a surreal Paris that few tourists ever encounter."
—*Library Journal*

"Replete with literary exoticism, [Osborne's] writing is...lush, a cornucopia of exploding images."
—*The Times* (London)

LAWRENCE OSBORNE
PARIS DREAMBOOK

Lawrence Osborne's other books include *The Angelic Game* and *Ania Malina*. He has lived in Paris for many years.

Paris Dreambook

An Unconventional Guide to the Splendor and Squalor of the City

LAWRENCE OSBORNE

Vintage Departures
Vintage Books
A Division of Random House, Inc.
New York

FIRST VINTAGE DEPARTURES EDITION, JUNE 1992

Copyright © 1990 by Lawrence Osborne

Library of Congress Cataloging-in-Publication Data
Osborne, Lawrence, 1958–
Paris dreambook: an unconventional guide to the splendor
and squalor of the city / Lawrence Osborne.
—1st Vintage Departures ed.
p.   cm. — (Vintage departures)
Originally published: London : Bloomsbury, 1990.
ISBN 0-679-73775-8 (pbk.)
1. Paris (France)—Guidebooks.   I. Title.
[DC708.O83   1992]
914.4'3604839—dc20   91-50709
CIP

Author photograph © Marie-Paule Galiana

Hand Lettering by Anne Scatto

Manufactured in the United States of America

10 9 8 7 6 5 4

Forever-obliging friends in Paris:
Luisa Maisel and Xavier de Montrand,
Chris Cross and Marie-Paul Galiana,
Nicole Lambert and Cyril de Turkheim.

A dream about the nakedness of man imprisoned
in the most bizarre, the most atrocious clothing . . .

W. Gombrowicz,
from Preface to *Operetta* (1967)

Contents

PARIS DREAMBOOK

Since the beginning of its history, Paris has drawn to it that dubious and pathetic figure, the peasant. Over the centuries, the dreaming provincial has provided the City's literature with some of its most enduring and subversive characters, from Restif de la Bretonne's roaming peasant, cousin of the 'Owl' who stalked the metropolis's streets during the Revolution in search of adventure and curiosity, to Louis Aragon's surrealist rustic dreaming his way through the self-transforming city of the 1920s. Consciously or otherwise, every modern migrant to the City undergoes the inner turbulence of these imaginary peasants. And the peasant, invented over and over again in the evolution of this savage and satirical tradition, becomes a figure as eternal as the fool or the knight. He is, as Aragon said, the subconscious of urban man and therefore the hidden author of his catastrophic dreams.

Following this same tradition, the preferred medium of the modern peasant can only be the fantasy journal that has served him well already. Always wary of elevated comparisons, however, more often than not he pretends to be a miserable and wretched solitary prowling haphazardly on the hazed peripheries of his adopted city. He regards himself as a noble leper skulking in the shadows. All he has, or so he says, is a pen, a pile of paper and the untrustworthy cerebral organ in which he is always free to write one more bucolic dreambook.

Equipped, then, with all the necessary precedents – and armed with the literary forms, topographical preparations and mental delinquency he will need – he sits down and begins his work.

The Loss of the City

✛

At first there was no sound as the water rose from the drains, lapped over the kerbs and restaurant doors, spilled untidily into the underground stations and filled up the cavities between the platforms. It came in tides streaked with what looked like Purple of Cassius, carrying a cargo of rats, crates of cabbages and uprooted plastic seats. Within minutes the gongs were sounding in the workers' quarters, the sirens were wailing and, as the sewers cracked and disgorged their contents into the tide, the voices of hysterical female officials were heard on the loudspeakers: 'Citizens of the future, be so good as to do your duty with your buckets! All workers to the municipal pumps!' But as the pylons collapsed, the City was plunged into darkness. And as the oily slime made its way into shops, garages and *concierges'* lounges the population took themselves screaming to the roof tops. Everywhere, clinging to makeshift rafts, scampering like rodents up church façades and famous monuments, the people fled the rising water, which now glowed with vagrant chemicals, until they stood perched like forlorn and abandoned lemmings upon the tips of the City's highest points, surrounded and immobilized: waiting to jump! But the tide, in all its imperturbable viciousness, had no intention of stopping there.

It rose further, inch by inch. The power stations on the edge of the City exploded and floated skyward. The people, in their desperation for their culture to survive, hauled gramophone records, shelves of books, books of reproductions and whole pianos to the roof tops. The death of the City! The wished for and the unthinkable.

And as the City finally went under, all except for the proud tip of the Eiffel Tower, suddenly, from nowhere, seeping out of the eerie waterscape of the drowned metropolis as if orchestrated by gleeful angels, there came a sound of music. Yes, there was no

mistaking it, the dying survivors could hardly believe their ears
. . . the St Matthew Passion!

The slime stopped and momentarily held its breath.

As the City died, the existence of God was finally proved.

The peasant on the train passing through the northern suburbs
of this same City wakes as suddenly as he fell asleep and rubs
his eyes. The City is not dead, the suburbs have not disappeared
under a lake of chemically poisoned sludge and the little villas
with their industrial ceramic decorations and trimmed gardens of
limp bougainvillaea are still there. He might have breathed a sigh
of relief, but in truth his bucolic bigotry is stubborn, tempered as
it has been by the myths of apocalyptic science fiction. He merely
bites his lower lip in disappointment. On the horizon, silhouetted
cranes poke like marsh birds among a maze of concrete weeds
and he sees that the blue and pink neon signs are still there, as
they always are at dusk, standing watch over the aborigines.

The truth is that our hero, our innocent peasant, is a virulent
rustic despite no evidence of calluses on his hands and despite
not wearing a pair of curling wooden clogs. He watches with
disbelief, and with rising dyspepsia, the crazy Gothic houses fly
by, fantastical gables dark with soot, machicolations, shutters,
brickwork, Swiss chalets, gingerbread mini-castles topped with
turrets and narrow vertical villas crowned with bizarre combs of
chimneys . . . an industrial museum stretching to the horizon
in all directions. The urban museum is being switched on for the
night. Its houses full of ghosts are stirring sluggishly into life.

The peasant counts them: Argenteuil, a second Nagasaki; the
Ile des Ravageurs, last resting place of Paris's Fifis and Cigars;
Enghien, the shadow of a nineteenth-century gambling town;
Aubervilliers, the Red Belt. The passengers are still asleep, but
if they were awake the names would be no more familiar to them
than the names of small Inca garrison towns. The suburbs sink
under their lights, even deeper into ash-covered anonymity. The
peasant stops counting.

Factories, vast lots filled with thousands of identical cars; turns
in the river: the City is getting nearer.

The water has the oily black colour of balsam of Peru.

The streets are now as bright as neon Osglim lamps.

An Egyptian blue sky recedes into a darkness crossed with clouds of Dutch metal and the City flares up around the train with the violence of a naphtha fire. Perhaps the peasant is nervous as he sits there watching this explosion of light erupt below him, but then isn't he prepared for the death of the City, an event which he is convinced, for purely mythic reasons, is imminent? Like all peasants, for him the death of the City is as inevitable as it is unthinkable. He is secretly waiting for it to happen. And the City makes him nervous as it approaches because against all the odds it is still alive and palpitating with the beats of a hidden heart. Its arteries still teem with millions of corpuscles. Its bones are still buried under flesh. Its stomach still heaves with acids.

The death of the City is incomplete, but none of the passengers has yet woken to verify the good news. The northern *arrondissements* appear to be burning without an audience. It is only as the train pulls into the last half-mile of track shadowed by tall embankments in the approach to the Gare St Lazare that their eyes begin to flicker and pop open. And, blinking slowly, they then see nothing which surprises them.

But the peasant is in a state of fever. The run in reminds him of a gas chamber. He struggles to control his claustrophobic excitement. Within seconds of the train coming to a halt, he is in the streets, having dashed down the side exit on to the rue d'Amsterdam, but once there – having successfully avoided the station's massive Age of Industry vaults bedecked with gaudy pennants and ad-panels and, even better, the disorganized plaza in front of the façade – he is paralysed with confusion. He wants only one thing before the City dies: to escape.

Desperate for this therapeutic release from his own paralysis, he loses no time in crossing the street, following it down to the rue St Lazare, which crosses it at right angles, and charging left down the latter.

But the rue St Lazare is not secretive enough to rescue him. He searches for another, smaller exit from it. He is determined to enter the City by means of as many accidental turnings as possible. And before he has gone more than a few paces he has suddenly found the entrance to a suffocating alley that climbs downwards in an unknown direction: he has stumbled upon the Métropolitain.

He dives down the cloistered stairs and feels a sweet and exotic odour being sucked into his head. Without knowing it, he has penetrated the Metro, the most parochial and secluded asylum for lost souls in the City. And it is in the Metro, that lugubrious and dynamic enclave of extra-marital relief, cocaine-scented corridors and African atrapas, that Fata Morgana of vice, that the peasant first steps out of his rustic skin and into the luminous organism of the City.

His heart is beating violently.

He is already reaching for meagre banknotes.

But his head is serene and free from gravity.

For the first time in his life – as if maliciously brought to life by a playful jinn – it has begun to dream efficiently.

Metroworld

✚

In Paris the public transportation system does not bear a vernacular name, it is not the 'Underground' or the 'Subway' or the 'Unterbahn': it is the Metro, the Métropolitain. A word as Greek as the word cosmopolitan. In fact, the system could easily have been called the Cosmos, since the names of its stations pretend to encompass the entirety of human history, defining as they do a mental geography that contains battlefields, poets, entire nations, capital cities, revolutionaries, animals and scientists. A lithe and elastic cosmopolitanism shines through the city in the names of its Metro stations, all of which share in the dream of the Universal City.

The Metro is above all a system of names, names which are a thousand times more secretive than the places they supposedly denote. Filles du Calvaire, Bel-Air, Crimée, Danube, Pyramides, Campo-Formio, Botzaris, Croix-de-Chavaux, Jasmin, Ourcq . . . the mercurial names of the Metro, with the exoticism of the names of extinct birds and buried cities. The three most mysterious to the foreign ear are Exelmans, Télégraphe and St Ambroise, which are ascetic and distant, like the white hills upon which monasteries are built. Extravagantly politicized and willing to whisper propaganda, catholic and Catholic, ready to act as stele to Great Men, palimpsestic and hermetic, the Metro names will be remembered in the future as a schoolchild's mnemonic for the ancient history of Europe or as a crazy hieroglyphic inscription over which scholars will shake their heads as dubiously as they once did confronted with the walls of Luxor. Why, they ask, was Stalingrad included in the same city as Austerlitz, why was Bolivar thrown in with Charles de Gaulle, St Sebastian with Marx – and where is Napoleon? A station for George V and Garibaldi but not Napoleon! Incredible self-effacement in the name of the spirit of the

11

Metro! It will be concluded, of course that the Metro was an idea, a religious idea, perhaps, or a pan-humanitarian one, but never a public transport system. That would be like saying the pyramid of Djerber was an ancient shopping mall. The Metro was an idea in the mind of twentieth-century man and the astrological map around which his archaic spirituality revolved. In it he tried to express his yearnings for unity and harmony in the face of the chaos of his history, and if people wished to drive around in trains along the configurations appointed by this divine map of reality that only shows how deeply the people of this age felt their pan-humanistic rituals. This undoubtedly explains why the system did not run in straight lines. What do straight lines have to do with enlightenment?

And the passengers on the Metro themselves are subject to various forms of wild daydreaming as they pass along the intertwining lines like Aborigines feeling their way along songlines. *En route* from Tolbiac to Brochant, from Corentin-Coriou to St Mandé-Tourelle, from Marcel Sembat to Garibaldi, they gradually lose their sense of reality, bombarded as they are by hailstorms of associations evoked by the Metro's melodic names. The voyager travelling to Argentine or to Danube thinks, if only for seconds, of phantasmagoric pampas, tangos, strange-looking cowboy hats and snobs dancing waltzes in the warm evenings of the nineteenth century . . . barbaric images of history telescoped into millions of heads every day, countless times every minute of every day, and all because of these names dreamed up in the spirit of agnosia and urban philanthropy. Nowhere on earth is so much expendable dreaming occasioned by so much inadvertent linguistic exoticism. The Metro is a masterpiece of literature.

The Metro is best at night. After dark it loses its inhibitions and complexes and becomes as whorish as it is meant to be. The brilliant combustion of electricity in the air, the proliferation of gleaming surfaces and the artificial brightness of everything underground reminds you of the make up of a successful tart while giving to the skins of its clients the pale hue of troglodytes. It is now that the prudent user of the world's finest underground transportation system can best exploit its innate tendency towards dream. The multifarious races of the City's patchwork of peoples merge and blend against their will, and it has been known for some passengers at night to enter one station white and exit by another black, and vice versa. Not without a smile you remember the strange deaths that people meet underground – the general, for example, in the Metro's first years who died when his beard was caught in the new-fangled automatic doors, or the tramp stabbed in a frenzy by a well-heeled commuter who leaped across the tracks knife in hand in order to punish some drunken foul language. You remember the Aboriginal crowds of frustrated rush-hour passengers who during the strike marched *en masse* from station to station along the live rails lynching RATP staff *en route*, behaving in ways that would have been impossible in the other Paris, the city up in the air. Apprehensively, you remember the Morlocks who lived underground and fed on the reservoirs of white flesh from the upper world. You look more closely at the faces around brutalized by the mere fact of being underground.

However, like our peasant, you are resolved to indulge in Metro dreams and so you direct yourself to a station suitably conducive to the necessary initial suspension of disbelief. An admirable station for this purpose is Vaneau on the rue de Sèvres because outside, despite the overall smallness and shabbiness of this quiet stop on the Boulogne-Austerlitz line, it has the virtue of being equipped with a life-sized Egyptian water-carrier set into the wall by the entrance, the same wall that encircles the Hôpital Laennec. The blank gaze of this haunting statue gives rise in your mind, as you go down the steps, to the conjecture that Paris was once an Egyptian city, as can otherwise be confirmed by visiting the Place du Caire, with its crazy pharaonic heads set into the walls. This might at least be true of the Metro which is, despite what historians will tell you, by far the most ancient part of the city. Under the influence of this presentiment you look for and indeed find the hieroglyphs you have been expecting etched along the tunnels with spray cans and seeming to spell the English word 'shark' *ad infinitum*. The décor of the Vaneau station does not bring you down to earth, either, although admittedly it is less Egyptian than you had hoped. There is, for example, the tramp who is always asleep at night on the Austerlitz platform within a circle of orange peel, beer bottle tops, arcs of frozen saliva and fragmented teeth . . . he may be imitating the recumbent posture of a mummy, but you can tell he is alive by the curling of his naked toes. And then the advertisements pasted the length of the curved walls within ochre-yellow scrolled frames.

We are aware of the temptation to cheap and anti-capitalistic moralisms against the publicity in the Metro – where its presence is, it seems, most lamented. But let us say straight away that we are not indignant about it, nor are we moved to noble fury at the thought of the slow but irresistible degradation of our finer instincts by these profit-orientated buffooneries. Quite the contrary: we are in favour of these giant posters being made compulsory by law in all public places, and above all in all Metro stations. They are the outposts of the unconscious in the domain of public transport and as such should be rigorously imposed upon all urban travellers and visitors, whatever their supposed political preferences. For example, let us take the coffee ads. True, they are a little spoiled by their pseudo-sexual logos: every one of them seems prepared to copulate with the consumer. Douceur Noire, the language of desire. Café Grand-Mère, the Arabica that strokes the drinker's scrotum while raping his epiglottis. Copacabana, the taste of creole thighs and aroused armpits. The texts are designed to elicit loathsome and reactionary responses in the regions of the lower bowels. And not one of them compares say the taste of Lavazza with the pleasures of a fishing trip, a toboggan ride, a Beethoven concerto or a spring day in the Appalachians. No, it is all orgasm, licking, sighs and satin slips. While this might offend the odd revolutionary, it has to be admitted that the images that go with these banal texts are viciously seductive: the pair of dark hands filled with coffee beans surging out of a tropical blue sky with a globose orange moon and the shadowed tips of palm trees; a white hand loitering with intent against the black rump of an evening dress suggesting a drop of cream in an espresso; a pair of cochineal lips working their way around a teaspoon while a vaguely female rose of the same colour sulks on a saucer and a limp male mouth implants itself on the left cheek of the owner of the lips. Who can deny that these compositions, which suggest in no uncertain terms what will happen to you if you happen to drink coffee in conjunction with your favourite contraceptive on an evening when the moon is full, are infinitely preferable to the bloated faces of tabby cats gorging themselves on piles of excretal high-fibre tunny-flavoured nuggets, or those of enamelled cocottes gulping down whole bottles of drinkable active-ingredient yogurt? The founder of the Metro, Fulgence Bienvenue, made the following remark: 'In another age the appearance of the Metro would have given rise to a special and particular mythology'; but isn't it truer to say that that mythology has already come to pass and that its heroes, impossible animals, demons and beauties are already elevated to the status of Elgin Marbles in the form of the station ads? The Metro is already a giant brain sleeping through decades of history and filled with endless unrepeatable nightmares.

The neurons and nodes of this catastrophic dreaming organ are the 429 stations, 80 kilometres of corridor and 295 kilometres of track. And like any brain it is filled with heroes and villains. From the beginning of its active life at the turn of the century it has been capable of inflicting both terror and romance upon its users. Despite the hysteria of the contemporary moralist, who sees in the everyday manners and rising crime of the Metro the beginnings of the disintegration of an entire civilization, it has always harboured peripatetic sadists, Dalinian exhibitionists, lone avengers like the Woman in Black with her sinister sharpened needle who terrorized the network more than half a century ago, the *apaches* of the Belle Epoque and its armies of homeless tramps. Its crimes are peculiar to it, whether they be the hold up of a train at Anvers station by Fantômas and the drugging of its passengers, who are later found wandering dazed and aimless around the City, or those prosaic but unsolved murders that rise to the surface of the Metro's dreaming mind like nefarious and misformed flowers.

Of all the murders committed on the Metro in the dubious realm of historical fact, the most mysterious and typical is the assassination at the Porte Dorée in 1937. On May 16th of that year a young woman got on to a Metro train at the Porte de Charenton station on what is now the Balard-Créteil line in the direction of Bastille. She was noticed by the staff because of a decorative ribbon awarded to her by a charity to which she belonged. At 6.30 pm the train stopped at Porte Dorée, the next station on the line. The young woman, whose name turned out to be Yolande-Laetitia Tourneaux, was found on the floor of the compartment with a knife half-protruding from her neck. She was still alive, and a policeman called to the scene was able to remove the blade from her neck before she was taken to hospital. She died in the ambulance. The sensational crime attracted nationwide attention. A Commissaire Badin was assigned to the case but made no headway. The killer had escaped and the policeman had effaced vital finger traces from the weapon. Over the weeks, however, the press made even more sensational revelations about the seemingly innocent Mlle Tourneaux. She had worked in a nightclub called the L'As de Cœur on the rue des Vertus and had occasionally been in the employ of a private detective agency run by a certain M. Rouffignac in the capacity of a freelance detective. It further transpired that she had been employed through Rouffignac to protect the Italian Embassy under the name of Nourissat. Murder suspects thus changed: anti-fascist underground cells, the Cagoulards, the various hit-men friends of Rouffignac, some of whom had frequented the L'As de Coeur. The press howled that the name was known but was being covered up by the government. And in fact the case was never solved, the murderer of the Porte Dorée was never found and the mythic power of the Metro, already so firmly entrenched in the lurid unconscious of the masses through the instruments of the media, deepened and darkened. The statistical knowledge that since its inception only 0·007 of travellers have died in the Metro through accidents or crime – and this includes the 400 killed on Line 9 on April 4th, 1943 by an Anglo-American bomb – does not loosen the hold of fantasy. As Kafka noted during his visit to Paris, in the Metro, 'one is an element of an urban installation, something like water in a conduit', and the presentiment of helplessness that afflicts the buried, enclosed human animal is comparable to the panic that seizes a calf in an abattoir.

From Vaneau, however, forgetting these alarming associations, you pass to Sèvres-Babylone, a station which holds no interest for you except in so far as the very word Babylon encapsulates the ancient anima of the Metro, and here you encounter the chief pleasure of these ingenious systems of subterranean transport: the freedom of individual choice. At Babylon, as in the real city, roads cross and the traveller is free to indulge himself as far as his destination (which is the same as his destiny) is concerned. North to adventures in the exotic and treacherous regions of the Carrefour Pleyel or St Lazare or east to the playgrounds of Cardinal Lemoine or St Michel. Of course, the traveller in search of some decent oneiric activity can only choose the Porte de Clignancourt line, which he can join at Odéon and which takes him through landscapes of convulsive disobedience. The trip may begin anodynely enough, but soon an equinoctial disequilibrium enters the carriages with the influx of barbarism associated with Les Halles and reaches a climax of disorder between Etienne Marcel and Barbès. It is best to take this line during a strike, when the other lines are unexpectedly closed and when the carriages are so full of lemming-like night creatures that you feel you are on a freight train of human cattle bound for Auschwitz – with all the possibilities for witnessing spontaneous explosions of violence and social tension that a train without brakes imagined by Céline crashing through a landscape of marshes and pill-boxes could offer. You will not, however, always be so lucky. When the doors open at Les Halles a fresh and intoxicating aroma of menace enters the carriages nevertheless and always a small gnome with scrofula, who begins expounding to the crowd the evils of unemployment, social-security administration procedures, the problems of feeding seventeen children or recovering from acute pyaemia and the necessity of transferring cash to his palm in exchange for haunting views of amazing scars traced over a belly distended by the ravages of lumbago. For it is in the Metro that the diseased of the City, having crawled heroically from their workhouse beds, reveal to a shocked and sympathetic public the evils of the supposedly superior metropolis above. It is only in the Metro that sociologists can observe the nation's silent lepers. It is only underground that the tentacular technological organ passing for the City's unconscious excretes its desperate and tragic human stools.

The Russian author Kalitsky begins his famous novel of the Moscow Metro (the only novel as far as we are aware that bears the simple title *Métro*) with some unflattering remarks about the Taj Mahal. People say, he observes, that the Taj Mahal is the most beautiful building in the world, whereas the truth is that nothing is in fact more ineffable, more spiritual or more mysterious than the Metro – even the word itself is more magical for him than the words Taj Mahal, which he feels he cannot pronounce properly.

The Metro, he explains, is a complete world, with its frontiers, social classes, economic system and ancestral memories, and it is possible to see certain alcoholics mount at Arbat station on the circular line and stay on the train from dawn to midnight without for a minute missing the open air, the greenery of public parks or the sound of birds in the trees. No, for them the life subterranean is perfect. In this respect the Metros of Moscow and Paris are identical. Their functionalism has been repealed. The original *édicules* of Guimard covering the station entrances, with their organic and undulating green ribs derived from the moralism of Ruskin and the nature worship of Horta, set from the first moment of descent the tone of anti-industrial romanticism. That poignant art nouveau colour, green, is not incidental. The sentimental illusions of future peasants were, it seems, borne in mind by the original architects of industrial civilization's greatest public amenity.

It is with some surprise, not to say outrage, that you discover there are no trees on the platforms or sprouting between the lines. Similarly, the orange and white neons and *le Tube* video screens showing morsels of homogeneous cultural pap that brighten every platform seem completely heretical after the arborescent *édicules*. It is clear that the moral progress of the Metro is in fact going backwards, leaping into the foul arms, so you think, of the present age. Where is the fighting spirit of the Front National du Métro, which so gallantly aided the French Resistance? Where are the forgotten attempts to scent the underground system with lemon grass in the beautiful years before the First World War? Where are the ticket inspectors singing the music-hall song:

C'est pour le métro, métropoli, tropolitain?

Where are the wagons tacked on to the end of the trains reserved for the Jews under the Occupation and known popularly as 'The Synagogue'? Where is Fantômas and his chloroform? Where is the ghost of the half-decapitated Colonel Decharbogne, martyr to the cause of rubber linings on the doors? Where are the airplane parts factory at the Place de Fêtes and the stage sets of *Les Portes de la Nuit*? The answer is that they have been relegated to the dustbin of the past by the new MF77 trains with their blue plastic noses and by the insane passion for strip lighting, blow ups of bookish lithographs and plaster casts of museum exhibits in dainty cases, life-size reproductions of Rodin sculptures and permanent educational mini-exhibitions on subjects such as 'The Water You Drink' and 'How Nuclear Energy Warms Your Bath'.

Enough is enough, you say to yourself in disgust, and concentrate your whole attention upon the giant faces of computer-registered *putes* and the stream of real faces that succeed in subverting the management's attempts at rationalization and which are the source of your continual pleasure. You could swear, as a matter of fact, that you see the same faces day after day. The Nefertiti, for example, always getting off at Madeleine and always winking at you as she sweeps down the platform; the snoring head of the banjo player on his way to Strasbourg-St Denis who always magically wakes up when his station has arrived, his little gipsy nose partially eaten away by some epithelial cancer; the various physiognomies of Ramapithecus Man flashing across screens of empty air lit by the ubiquitous and sickening electricity – a light as virile as an endless photographic flash and which burns them into the memory with an insolent and persuasive violence; and most of all the old man who plays Italian songs on a mandolin in the long corridor at Sèvres-Babylone and whose begging cap never contains any coins except what our peasant, who enjoys his bad but heart-breaking playing, gives him.

You conclude that the Metro is a machine for processing faces, crossing and combining them, spewing them out senselessly in all directions and that it might have been more effective if the advice of the Ligue Parisienne du Métro Aerienne, which campaigned in the 1890s for an overhead instead of an underground system, had been heeded after all. For the only time when this monstrous discharge of disorientated faces becomes human once more, alert to its surroundings and suffused with some vaguely biological colour, is when the train shoots up from underground into the open air, borne up by the elegant and gay iron-vaulted overpasses whose supporting pillars are embellished with all kinds of anachronistic cartouches, scrolls, fluting and sculpted garlands. It can only be regretted that this Jules Vernian conception of the Metro, with its joy in technically advanced acts of levitation and naïve show-off bravura, was buried by the earnest Vulcian school of engineers content to work sombre and forbidding miracles underground. It is possible, of course, that in the future the system will be filled up with sand and the overhead bridges extended to cover the entire City, while the style of the confident and tasteful *avante-garde* of 1895 is retained so that, by a conscious act of municipal remembrance, a vast megalopolis of gravity-induced vehicles will circulate around, beneath and next to a network of neo-Grecian pillars and romantic shadows. But, let us admit immediately, the chances of this happening in the vertigo of Futuropolis are as likely as the invention and mass-marketing of immortality. The travelling human unit will become more subterraneanly orientated, the human complexion will pale even further in response to a necessary deprivation of ultra-violet rays and the physiognomy of the human face will grow more vegetal, chilling and blank. We can only cross our fingers and hope that pornographic advertising will come to the rescue . . .

The other hope – one which frankly gives us the greatest sense of expectation and proleptic titillation – is the possibility that Fantômas will resurrect himself and commit an act of terrorism so great, so scandalous, so inadmissible and so useless that the days of mass hysteria will be brought back and the adventure of underground restored to its former virility. Nor should you smile at this childish and quaint idea. For if the Metro is the city's unconscious, its slumbering, nightmare-filled brain, its perpetual darkened bedroom where dreams go unhindered for decades and eventually centuries, then like any oversized head it can create any incubus it likes, nothing can stop it piling up lunacies . . . accidents and crimes, riots and epic arsons . . . even, if you like, a call-girl at the end of the line at midnight, although in this case you will never know for as you approach your destination, drooling with lust, you are suddenly overwhelmed by another desire altogether, one that has been conferred upon you by the closeness and sweatiness of the Metro itself, which always seems to be overheated, a desire which brusquely makes you forget all about your precious rendezvous and all it might have promised: namely to visit a Turkish bath. You needn't feel ashamed to want to plunge yourself into a hammam – on the contrary, our peasant feels exactly the same thing every time he takes a trip on the Metro. After all, the two experiences are not dissimilar, with the difference that the latter is infinitely more narcotic. But before heading impulsively back to the surface and charging into no matter which establishment you may happen to find on your path, you would be well advised to read attentively the following chapter, which, apart from providing a few enlightening principles, general observations, wide-ranging and thoughtful meditations on the nature of bathing and steam rooms, and poetic descriptions of every stage of hammam relaxation, also supplies some useful addresses and practical tips concerning the Turkish baths of this remarkably heteroclite city where the masseurs are equal to those of Istanbul and where the steam of its underground baths is as densely scented with eucalyptus as those of Fez or Cairo.

A Short Guide to Turkish Baths

It is almost certain that the Arabs learned the secrets of the art of public bathing, with its meditative and homoerotic dimensions, from the four hundred bath houses of the Alexandria they conquered. In the modern equivalent of Alexandria the Islamicized art of corporeal purification has come home to roost in the city where the largest Roman ruin is a municipal bath and in which the desire for solitude is so intense that its ultimate gratification may rest only with the *hammam aturki,* the *bain Turc.* Our peasant, now that some months have passed and he is firmly established as a naturalized citizen of the City, has become so addicted to this far from gratuitous pastime that he spends almost all his money on the joys of steam rooms, refrigerated pools and the manic manual skills of the little Maghrebian masseurs who can be picked up almost as easily as street girls and for a fraction of the cost. A light and intensely individual eroticism holds court in the depths of the hammam in almost alarming harmony with a communal serenity enforced by the habit of the masseurs in the smaller establishments of interrupting all operations at five o'clock precisely, unwrapping their wicker mats between the massage tables in the direction of Mecca and offering up their devotions in quiet but heartfelt undertones. The object of the hammam is to escape the City and the world around it. Not only does the Moslem, as in the mosque, escape the City of War, but the sensual atheist, too, escapes from the asphyxia of the present and exiting by a series of illusionist doors in the form of underground chambers and ante-chambers, of mystic waters and fountains, leaves his existence behind, flirts more openly than ever before with his own body and suffers a sudden and vertiginous loss of toxicity – a brutal advent of cleanliness that leaves him in a state of memoryless disorientation for hours and even days afterwards.

The Turkish bath, with its mystique derived from the tendency of the European to indulge in infantile fantasies of the opulent, promiscuous, sorbet-eating East, the East of exemplary consumerist living which was never actually observed from close to, retains – in the high-class tourist establishments at least – the aura of the opium-smoking 1920s. The guides who cater to well-heeled international itinerants or local businessmen, the Gault-Millau for example, do not hesitate to include sections on the Turkish baths and the baths which they recommend are all devoid of true alien content, with the notable exception of the glorious hammam of the Mosquée de Paris. They are approximations to the original which compromise with Scandinavian modes of ablution. The systems of massage used, for example, with their – to our mind – tame and unimaginative hand-chopping and shoulder-kneading (as opposed to the more athletic and strenuous tendon-wrenching of the masseurs of the Middle East), seem to us to be entirely heretical in the context of the true hammam, as are their inclusion of such contraptions as saunas, exercise bicycles, vegetarian restaurants and bars. Let us be as explicit as possible: the true hammam is not a health club or a glorified gym. It is a place of non-activity, of withdrawal. The slightest athletic movement spoils the peculiar spiritual density of the small rooms, where every occupant is aware of every other down to his fingernails and the trails of sweat moving down his spine. Slowness of movement and reaction, a dropsical detachment, enable the bather to feel intimate with his fellow sufferers and to feel a primitive sympathy for his greatest defects, even for the rolls of diseased fat, the distended and craven bellies, the shrivelled-up penises that tempt bravura – or, for that matter, for his greatest points of superiority, for the baths sometimes throw up disciplined and poetic male bodies that move with the ease of hammerhead sharks and which restore the dim memory of Roman court favourites, Neronic love-boys and professional Adonises expert in the nibbling of imperial testicles.

An example of the hammam that has missed its destiny is the Hammam St Paul on the rue des Rosiers in the Marais. It might have been difficult, of course, to maintain a scrupulous Moslem profile in this Jewish neighbourhood, with kosher butchers and cinnamon-scented bakeries filled with seven-armed candelabra only a few doors down, and the façade itself betrays other points of origin: the gold mosaic lettering set into a chocolate wall and sculpted lions' heads on either side of a window with a blue push-out blind are clearly affected with 1930s mannerisms. A cramped lobby downstairs in a quaintly rectilinear style provides you with a staircase leading up to the first-floor restaurant and reception area housing a bar, a large and sunny space with rows of empty tables, rubber plants and semi-recumbent male forms draped in white bath towels. Subtending to this area are the mauve cubicles reminiscent of an obsolete swimming pool and from here, after undressing in distressing and anaemic solitude, you descend the stairs to the baths. A crude thermal titillation awaits you. You sweat even before you push open the door that leads into the nondescript showers and by the time you have penetrated one set of doors further into the hexagonal steam lounge – the purgatory between the hell of the full steam room and the paradise of the ice-cold pool in the central atrium – your armpits are thrashing about in a swelter of racing moisture, you are reeking, your heartbeat has tripled, your eyeballs are popping like fragile ceramic objects accidentally thrown into a roaring oven. In this gasping, vapid little room long spruce deckchairs are ranged around a circular table of the same wood bearing a variety of French newspapers. You are intended to seat yourself, prevent yourself from passing out by checking the dairy odours emanating from your boiling skin, and leaf through one of these soggy and glutinous journals with nimble fingernails.

It is not intended that you should be able to stand much of this sly thermic sadism and so it is that before long you desire to change direction and mood and – why not? – temperature. On either side of the door from the showers are the sauna and the steam bath. We would sincerely recommend you not to waste time in the sauna, which is naturally indistinguishable from all other saunas, and whose dry heat we find unbearable: direct yourself to the left-hand door and plunge into the inferno of the herbal steam room, where the moans of the dying are Dantean and where you can sit on any one of the ascending steps that recede back into invisibility behind the wall of vapour, each one getting hotter as it gets nearer the ceiling. The heat here is abusive, the burning combustion that can be imagined on the surface of a wretched moon of Jupiter, except that here the steam is scented with eucalyptus and a piercing and tonic freshness quickly fills the lungs. The only criticism that can be levelled against this exemplary steam room, which is properly sealed at the correct temperature, is that far from our much-awaited ideal of repose and abstraction we find here fat businessmen discussing their sad little scandals in voices only half hushed and farting at regular intervals.

Needless to say, such vulgar interruptions are highly distressing to our refined and aristocratic peasant and you too may well find yourselves leaving prematurely and searching out the cold bath in order to attain your Sufic ecstasies. But you would be well advised to wait until you are on the verge of unconsciousness before making a move, and then you should move quickly, stride with closed eyes through the reading area, push through the aluminium doors into the atrium (which is cool and distinguished) and, ignoring the notices in 1930s demotic advising you not to hurl yourself about, hurl yourself into the small pool, at the bottom of which a multitude of tiny blue and white checked tiles dazzles the eye. You should be aware, of course, that this brusque but exquisite gesture, given the size of the pool and the room, will drench every occupant of every chair around you, but unlike the true hammam a certain egoism is permissible here. In any case, the atrium (for want of a better word) will now allow you to dry off in relative anonymity, being equipped with foam mats ranged along a raised dais on either side of the pool and here you can contemplate the hexagonal cupola cut into the ceiling in clear reference to its Andalusian model, the Roman clock presiding over the pool, the unfortunate and completely inappropriate photo-murals of Hawaian beaches and the plethora of yellowing notices on the walls arguing for silence, respect and cleanliness. Here, the same businessmen who irritated you in the steam bath come out gasping for air, brutally naked and half-boiled, and lower themselves quietly swearing into the icy water. You can see that they have difficulty breathing. They have the appearance of flabby consuls of the late empire, addled with erysipelas, or St Anthony's Fire. So they wheeze and disport themselves like wounded dolphins in the blue and white shimmer of the pool and the clock ticks slowly while you sleep in the shadow of the arcade on your foam bed and hours pass by in the continual migration from steam to water, from heat to cold, from moaning to gasping, from sickness to health. After a while you notice that you have begun to smell differently, a smell of foul yogurt that comes with the exposure of your inner filth. It is time for that modern necessity, soap, and you can only regret that the masseurs available here, and who cost an additional forty francs to the ninety you have already paid, are not authentic despite the fact that they soap you down as they should. You will have to go into the shower and do it yourself.

The truth is, we are not convinced that for ninety francs we are experiencing the hammam at its most disconcerting and gratifying. In fact, our peasant rarely consents to part with ninety francs at the St Paul unless he feels the need for the cold swimming pool – admittedly a luxury at most hammams. Depending on the area he finds himself in, there are numerous alternatives that remind him more of the hammams he has crawled through in the cities of North Africa, and more particularly of the exquisite massages he has enjoyed in the cheap unmarked bathhouses of Meknes and Fez, where the hot flagstones touched in the dark, the powerful hands of masseurs, the overpowering heat of underground vaults, produced in his mind the most powerful memories of all his various travels across the globe. His passion for these places was born in these distant cities and has mostly been prosecuted ever since on the margins of deserts, where the poignance of the public bath – the most potent and rich symbol of urban civility and utility – is at its greatest faced with the puritanism of the nomad. It was here that he discovered his distrust for the nomad, the scorner of bath-houses and therefore of libraries.

As in Alexandria, the hammam is the pivotal point of urbanity. It is the place where accumulated surplus time is spent and where the equivalent excess of eroticism is displayed and dissipated without action or violence. How significant that it is at the heart of the Islamic world that the hammam has imposed itself, as much at the centre as the much-vaunted mosque: that heart which is contested by, on the one hand, the classical urban tradition of intellect, leisure, tolerance and development and, on the other, the nomad pastoral tradition of disruption, perpetual violence, ascetic scorn, military rigour and social fluidity . . . the whole gamut of desert puritan values so glorified by Ibn Khaldun for the sake of its austerity and moral purity, but which can only destroy the precious fabric of the hammam, refusing to recognize as it does anything but the sterility of the moving man. In this way, invisibly seduced by our own desert jeremiads, our whining nomadism in the form of a thirst for the purity of the primitive, we see the Turkish bath as a locus for unparalleled sybaritic corruption, for discreet copulations and the begetting of illegitimate children. The fate of the bath in the life of the European city reflects this prejudice. Contrary to our myths of the Middle Ages, public bathing was popular in the European cities of the fourteenth century. The Church's edicts against 'washing', so beloved of those desiring to prove in the most irrefutable way the pitiful backwardness and barbarism of this otherwise irritatingly arrogant continent, turn out on closer historical inspection to be tirades against the bi-sexual public baths of which the German city of Augsburg contained dozens, eventually closed down on orders from the bishop and in which – men and women being entitled to rent private cubicles – a vast number of bastards were reported to have been sired. The Church did not care whether people were clean or not, it cared about their legitimacy. And yet the Church also, beyond its sense of spiritual responsibility, perpetuated the sneer of the original nomads, the greatest of whom is Moses. The urban mind of the Mediterranean, with its own fascination for the human body, only relinquished its bathroom habits under intense pressure from the outside, from the spiritual guerrillas of the desert. It seems to us, lying in the arcaded courtyards of the world's hammams, subdued by the bubbling of fountains and drowsily aware of the naked bodies propped against classical pillars and scraping oil from their arms, willingly immersed in the only form of collective masculinity devoid of aggression, in a calm enjoyment of architectural details, self-enclosing fraternity, absence of loud throats and locker-room wit, borne along by the immemorial forms of a relaxation that is eminently horizontal and silent, that we have returned to our Greco-Roman roots, however uproariously funny this may seem to fellow hyperboreans. Even the smallest Parisian hammam gives us this nostalgia – the 'pain of returning'.

There is, for example, the small place on the corner of the rue de Tombouctou and the Boulevard de la Chapelle in the Goutte d'Or, called El-Baraka but ominously missing from the telephone books. Situated between the railway lines fanning out behind the Gare du Nord which sprawl under the boulevard and a gaping hole at the angle with the rue de Chartres formed by the destruction of a block of tenements and which is now like a chalk quarry covered with gargantuan figures of street art, cubic skeletons and running gangsters depicted falling into the hole, the El-Baraka is announced by its delicate blue tiles and Moorish lancets rising unexpectedly out of the hurly-burly of the boulevard. A small neon sign is all that tells you there is not the usual Moroccan restaurant with whining lutes underneath. Instead, the vestibule is cramped, dark and hot and above all it is grave as all true hammams are. There is no joking and elbow-nudging here. The bath is a serious enterprise. For fifty francs you have a straightforward sweat and for a further twenty you can hire one of the two or three white-haired masseurs at the top of the stairs and take him down with you into the depths. The baths themselves are simple in the extreme: a shower and spotless defecation area, a long hot-room in dark blue tiles with basins set at regular intervals into the wall with a continuous bench running between them and, at the far end, properly screened by heavy plastic ribbons, the steam bath itself, a small triangular room in the same blue tiles. Despite the absence of extra luxuries the El-Baraka is a place of asylum. It is used only by the local Moslems, sandalled loan sharks, grocers scarrred with smallpox, oily clerics, students, train drivers, small-time landlords. It is an advantage of the familiarity that reigns in the El-Baraka that the attendants personally tie the knot in your bathrobe and in general speak to you with a certain outlandish deference. The drying and rest room, where the wet clients stretch out on their mattresses, has high mirhab-shaped windows giving on to the rue de Tombouctou and the boulevard – where the Metro trains crash along the overhead track – and lying between the walls of tiles in the heat of a burning afternoon while the myriad voices babbling in Arabic and Turkish on the suffocating boulevard seep into the silence of the baths, you know that you are no longer in the Paris of the glass towers and Napoleonic relics, you are in the Nilotic Paris, the Paris of Mesopotamia, the Flower of the Desert. And all this, at the Baraka, for fifty francs!

But whatever the advantages offered by the small baths of the

Goutte d'Or and however much our peasant resorts to them because they are in his neighbourhood, it cannot be denied that no hammam in Paris, or in the West, can equal in vertiginous decor and graceful eroticism the baths of the Paris Mosque situated on the Place du Puits de l'Ermite. Although we have made a resolution not to stray into descriptions of the tourist dimensions of the New Disneyland, we cannot help descending into the much-frequented and familiar Hammam of the Mosque, which is in addition charmingly attached to the tearoom where blow-dried nymphets and pouting schoolgirls with their quaint little Maghrebian pastries, tiny one-mouthful 'gazelle horns' and *keblahs*, oblivious to the fantastic world on the other side of the wall, where loin-clothed male bodies slump in an oleic dungeon of heat, where time moves slowly backward. As always, we have no idea what the female side of the baths is like, but here at least the ethos of the Ottomans ferments like yeast in the warmth. You wonder, in a moment of crass vulgarity, why there is not a mad Sultan spitting foam in one of its nooks and crannies or why at least there are no eunuchs in evidence – the calmness and luxury of the rest area with its veined marble columns and quietly murmuring fountain should be the ideal terrain for a multitude of obedient and heavily armed eunuchs . . .

Of all the secluded retreats which the City offers this is by far our favourite: the proliferation of geometric figures, assorted polygons, lozenges and stars in the painted wooden panels, the octagonal cupola opening up above the fountain, the dark red that predominates in the woodwork, the filtered light and the columns of the raised dais that surrounds the fountain on three sides are offset in the realm of sound by the steady murmur of the water sliding over the upper lip of the fountain and into the basin below, where bottles of water lie cooling. The dais is heated from below so that the tiles are always warm and mint tea is served with oranges to the reclining clients. Beyond the narrow doors that lead to the baths the décor is more Spartan and cavernous: white vaults brimming with condensation, raised alcoves framed with classical pillars with basins and taps where the stone flags are hot to the touch, the massage room with its single slippery bench and, in the middle room, an elegant central platform surrounded by columns with simply carved capitals bathed in a single shaft of light. The rooms become hotter progressively until at the far end you enter the final steam bath, a small chamber with, on the left, a raised platform and, on the right, a large circular cistern filled with sediments of grey clay. On the far side of the uncertain crater are two ventilators belching forth an agonizing heat. It is a point of masculine bravura to walk slowly around the cistern, passing within inches of the searing ventilators, with no gesture of disbelief except a casual wipe of the brow and it is an athletic achievement to do this even once without passing out and tumbling ignominiously into the cistern, from where you would be fished out covered in horrible and outlandish burns. Here the fat men do best, leaning on their thermostable guts and, for once, eyeing their thin rivals with contempt. They do not blush or quiver as the slim carcasses do; they absorb patiently like heat-seeking reptiles and the sweat that rolls off them is measured and wise. For those less endowed by nature with subcutaneous armour it will be necessary to retire quickly to the lesser steam room, where the basins are thoughtfully equipped with hoses attached to the cold-water taps.

The massages, by the axolotyl-like Hamid, are worth the fifty francs – but since you have only paid fifty-five francs to enter this stupendous hammam in the first place you will assume you have profited from a bargain. The massage is exactly as it would be anywhere in the Moslem world, since the movements are laid down according to physiologically tested ritual and are always executed with a methodical and patient exactitude. Contorting their bodies into bows, they stretch out the client from underneath by clasping his ankles and wrists, inflect his spine, pull the arms across the chest and move their hands along them as if squeezing a tube of toothpaste, displace each finger a millimetre from its joints, twist, thump, arch, distend, wrench, hiss and cluck. The service involves maximal effort on their part, using every part of their own body. Those so-called masseurs who content themselves with slapping a supine pair of shoulder blades with the sides of their hands seem worse than absurd by comparison. At the end of this gruelling set of figures the client feels broken apart, unstuck and magically reassembled. No ligament, tendon, muscle or nerve seems to have escaped the treatment. The spine, in particular, suffers a realignment suggestive of blissful fracture. At the same time the masseur oils and soaps the entire surface of the body with scrupulous attention to detail – although unlike the masseurs of the Maghreb they do not hurl buckets of scalding then cold water over it, much to our regret. The washing of the extremities of the fingers, carried through with such thoroughness, expresses an inadvertent tenderness which is communicated through the square, flattened nature of Hamid's toes and the similar bluntness of his fingers: through long hours of immersion in the tropical heat of the hammam they have become vegetal. They have the fibrous strength of tendrils of liana. You might well spend days of ecstasy in the Hammam of the Mosque, never quite able to tear yourself away from it through whole afternoons, as our peasant does (not only because he is indolent by nature but also because he can think of no better way to change identity). We might well suggest other hammams to you, the one next to the Chope des Artistes on the rue du Faubourg St Martin, for example, ensconced at the bottom of its grimy little passageway next to the Buzy Body clothes store, or the incredibly simple and secretive baths at 126 Avenue d'Italie announced by an old-fashioned black and gold sign – Bains et Hydrothérapie – and similarly hidden at the end of a run-down passage and courtyard which is truly in the middle of nowhere. But for the minimum price of around fifty francs it is impossible to improve upon the Mosque and nowhere else outside of the Goutte d'Or will the imperialism of the City be more easily disrupted. When will the day come when hammams are built on every street corner complete with muscly masseurs and carved *moucharabiehs*, polylobal arches and ceramic *zelliges*? When will the public bath drive out the fatuous private bathroom and regain the gigantism of Caracalla and Diocletian? When will the scent of scorched eucalyptus replace the obnoxious odours of shower gels and talcum powder? No doubt we are guilty once again of rash nostalgia of the past, but on this occasion we can claim the excuse that the hammam is not yet dead, that it thrives furtively under the City's skin and that one day it might just possibly erupt back into the national habits. When that happens the Age of Plenty will have returned to earth, the Golden Age, the Innocent Age, the Oh How Much Better It Was Age . . . the Age of the Turkish Bath.

But the hammams, as you slowly begin to realize, are only oases of peace in the livid organism of the City and like all oases they frame large tracts of desert between them. And one of these hostile Gobis of the Mind exists in all its terrifying largeness and imponderability inside the head of an ex-abattoir manager who lives on the third floor above the peasant's apartment at no. 37 rue André Antoine, who – as it happens – is right at this very minute having a ferocious dream about Genghis Khan and the Golden Horde. For M. Soufflet has something of an obsession with the Golden Horde. You see, they're going to come back one day, that old bastard Genghis Khan will come back too and destroy our beloved Paris . . . for everything is at risk, the barbarians are coming – indeed, they're already among us! – and it is only a matter of time before they start eviscerating children on the boulevards from the saddles of their stinking little ponies. It'll be like the Boches, only worse. The Mongols aren't even Aryans! And as history shows, the only thing they know how to do is wipe out cities, whole metropolises. Remember Baghdad, remember Delhi, remember Kiev! Curious to say, the pugnacious little ex-meat man has a moving and thoroughly noble attachment to the values of urban civilization and we can only listen with the utmost gravity to the dire warnings of his dreams . . . it is only to be regretted that M. Soufflet, in his hatred for everything alien, throws the baby out with the bathwater by associating the Mongols with Turkish baths. In this way we see that the curious nightmares inspired by the City leave no room for fine definitions. And M. Soufflet, fearing the contaminating breath of those ear-chopping goblins from the steppes, will never ever put a foot inside a hammam. There is nothing for him to do but suffer and dream.

Genghis Khan, Again

✠

In the year of Our Lord 1989, after the falling from Heaven of showers of frogs and sundry plagues of locusts and greenflies, a great noise was heard in the East: the wheel of history, turning slowly on its axis, threw the plains of Mongolia into turmoil and there arose a multitude of slit-eyed warriors assembled around the great felt tent of the re-born avatar, the ghost of Terror, the burning Genghis Khan risen from the dead. As innumerable as grains of sand the new Golden Horde re-entered the land of the Soviets, ripping up its cornfields, levelling its cities and impaling its citizens on wooden stakes. As irresistible as a human tidal wave, the horde overran Uzbekistan, poured into Georgia and the Ukraine and within a week was once again at the doorstep of the West. Tanks and nuclear missiles were useless against such cunning mobility, such sly and anachronistic genocide, such swift horsemanship! The Hungarians, the Poles, the Bulgarians all would have to relive the nightmare of their past. The trappings of stability fell away, chaos redescended upon the eastern half of the continent and the West assembled its armies as Budapest, Krakow and Sofia came crashing once more to the ground. And at the head of this invincible land-bound Armada of ponies, tents and totemic skulls rode the inscrutable Oriental face, lightly garnished with a refined moustache, of Genghis himself, the avenging fist of the gods.

Our M. Soufflet, hearing these stupendous tidings over the radio, immediately offered his services as a patriot volunteer in the Comité de Défence Nationale and its army of Home Guards raised among the civilian population, the latest manifestation of the dreaded *levée en masse* with which Parisian patriots have always tried to impress their enemies. At once he presented himself with his regulation pistol left over from the last war at the local Home

Guard offices in the church next door and was provided with a proud and masculine uniform in which he suddenly felt twenty years younger. At last, the day of reckoning with the hordes of Asia. At last, the chance to stick a bayonet, or worse, into the Yellow Peril! He never did approve of buying their tape recorders in the first place, and as for what they were doing with the drugs trade! But this was the final straw . . . now they were actually going to invade the country. *Aux armes, citoyens!*

As Citizen Soufflet made his way to the recruiting office, or rather as he dreamt that he was going to the recruiting office, he reflected on how, indeed, history seems to repeat itself. That great lead lion in the middle of the Place Denfert-Rochereau, for example, wasn't it a testimony to Paris's heroic resolve before the besieging armies of the East? Huns, Mongols, they were all the same. And didn't it appear that now just as then the City was rallying around the flag, the citizens were mobilizing to defend themselves against the barbarians as the citizens of Alexandria had once had to do and that just as in 1814, 1870 and 1940 the denizens of the City of Light would sober up, put on their uniforms and give the hordes from the far side of the Elbe a hard time of it? Not to mention the repulsion of the Huns back in the fifth century and the expulsion of the Goddams in the fifteenth. And what about Charles Martel? By the time he was in the recruiting office he was bursting with pride and courage. But, hardly was he in uniform than sensational news exploded out of nowhere: the Mongols, having crossed the Alps and massacred the entire Swiss nation with unspeakable cruelty, had arrived at the gates of Paris in a matter of hours! Living proof that it was they who had invented the tactics of *Blitzkrieg*!

The City was surrounded by an army of a million savages. From his embroidered tent Genghis Khan himself, flanked by his forbidding nephews among whom was the dreaded Hulagu, announced his terms as expected. Instant capitulation or the execution of the entire population of the twenty *arrondissements* and the dispatching of their ears in twenty thousand sacks to Karakorum. The dismantling of the Eiffel Tower, the conversion of the Sacré Cœur into a Mongol Pantheon and turning of the Tuileries into a huge stables and archery pit. The submission of all Parisian women to Mongol lust and the forcible introduction of Uigur as the official language in the schools. The abolition of paper money and the reintroduction of gold pieces, all of which were to be turned over to the Mongol army to be transported back in twenty thousand sacks to Karakorum. The destruction of the École Militaire and conversion of the Chambers des Députés into a giant felt tent reserved for the War Council of the Golden Horde.

Needless to say, these abominable and tyrannical terms were rejected by the government and so the Mongols began to catapult human heads into the city, along with naphtha balls, poisonous gas canisters and plague-ridden corpses. Strange to say, there also seemed no way of ending the blockade and before long the population was reduced, as in 1870, to eating rats and flying balloons. And just as in that earlier glorious campaign, the foremost minds of the Parisian universities set to work to devise secret weapons capable of smashing the enemy. Who had forgotten the ingenious machine, the 'musical machine-gun', that would crank out Schubert *lieder* to lure the cultured Boches out of their dug-outs and then mow them down as they were singing along? Who had forgotten the ingenious *escargots sympathiques* which would cross the enemy lines unnoticed bearing messages in their shells, or the *doigt prussique*, a needle dipped in acid with which the women of Paris would defend their virtue against the dirty Huns? Who had forgotten the incredible adventures of Paris's balloon aeronauts or the Amazons of the Seine in their black trousers? Not for nothing was there a lion in the Place Denfert-Rouchereau! Our man Soufflet ripped up paving stones like his ancestors to build barricades while the sky glowed red with fire and famine struck deep into the new Babylon. But already it was too late. The Mongols, by sheer weight of numbers, had forced a breach in the Home Guard's defences and were pouring into the holy streets of what Hugo had called the 'head of civilization'. Was it possible? Little men with slanting eyes? Bow and arrows, yellow skins, human sacrifices?

But the dream grew worse. The national defence was ineffective, the barbarian hordes let loose in the City were already committing their pagan atrocities. Half the City was on fire. The sound of alien tongues spread through the graceful streets of the metropolis. They killed wherever they felt like it, like that, in front of women and children, they looted the department stores, castrated the French paramilitaries with an insouciance bordering on contempt and tore down the tricolour wherever they found it still flying. In short, apocalypse! When they captured Montmartre they did not hesitate to re-enact the tragedy of the patriot Debray during the siege of 1814, the young man bayoneted and quartered by Russian troops and then stuck in four parts to the sails of the Blutefin windmill. They did exactly the same thing to another heroic member of the Resistance, only now the windmill is called the Moulin de la Galette. And who was the patriot so ignominiously paraded to the winds as a dismembered and defeated corpse resplendent in all his medals and his gay new uniform . . . why, our man Soufflet, who, dreaming the whole thing, was able to watch his own death at the hands of a band of Oriental thugs with mounting anguish and indignation. So there he was turning with the sails, blown around clockwise with one leg ridiculously separated from the other, his head stuck to the sail diametrically oppposed to his torso, his arms flailing uselessly in tune with the winds, with a splendid view over Paris, which he could see was burning, crumbling, screaming, smoking . . . what a way to die, Patriot Soufflet, quartered on a windmill on the fairest hill in Europe with a Mongol lance up your backside! How cruel is history when she is in a cynical and witty mood. How terse her little jokes are, how filled with cutting humour and anarchic pith! And in addition he was getting giddy, no, the turning of those damn sails didn't agree with him at all, it was time to wake up and see if all this nonsense was real after all.

With an effort tainted with disappointment and fury (he had genuinely hoped to turn the dream around and snatch a stunning victory from the jaws of defeat, just as General Trochu had hoped to during the Great Siege), he stopped the motion of the sails, re-assembled his poor body and, like a successful Humpty Dumpty, got down from the windmill without breaking himself up again. And as he got down he saw that, far from being a terrible and clear day in spring filled with blood and sunlight, it was night, the Mongols had gone – or had not yet arrived – that the *concierge* was snoring downstairs, the Brazilian faggots were grinding away on the ground-floor windowsills and that the Metro was roaring under the building causing the windows to vibrate lightly. Strange to say, he woke with a large erection and was filled with an almost uncontrollable lust such as often afflicts a dreamer waking from his reveries, however unpleasant these may have been. Rather pleased with himself he got dressed, unable to go back to sleep, and put on his outdoor shoes. As always when the human mind emerges from the hyperactivity of dream, M. Soufflet's brain would not let him off the hook: he had to do something, purge himself, satisfy his obscure craving for activity.

It was already midnight. Normally, the City settles into a relaxed rhythm in the early hours and it is only in a few highly charged places that the disappointed or rudely disturbed dreamer can find peace of mind in perpetual carnival. One of these places, no doubt the most claustrophic and unsettling of all, is the rue St Denis. Yes, for the M. Soufflets of this world, freshly roused from Mongol invasions, there is only one place to which to repair at the zero hour, when all else pales into triviality: the glorious serpent of a street where the only white nights south of Leningrad reveal the medieval heart of the City. The rue St Denis, or as our peasant knows it, the Carnival of Thighs. It is only here that the past surges up out of nowhere and takes the City by the throat; it is only here that it is the prostitute who makes the passer by feel abnormal and not the other way around. The rue St Denis is the nostalgic wound in the new Paris and one day, with the assistance of the proclivity of the urban mind for fragrant chaos, it will be strong enough to enter into open warfare with the City around it. And it should not be forgotten that, in the eventuality of the necessity of taking sides, half the City's population will desert her in favour of this single street, where the real is imperiously subdued by the grotesque, that essential component of human happiness. The fear of losing the grotesque will be too strong. The fear of losing happiness, nocturnal peccadilloes, the unsayable sin of whoring, the realm of the unspeakable which goes far beyond the act of exchanging money for oral sex, will be too great. The mind of the City clings to the rue St Denis as the hyperborean romantic clings to the promise of white nights.

White Nights at St Denis

Guides to the City are always obliged to make some mention of the rue St Denis. The conscientious tourist is advised to steer well clear of the City's most humid red-light district, or if he must pass through there, to wear an appropriate expression of disgust, embarrassment or sneering superiority riveted dutifully to his face. In this way he will be equipped with the right mask behind which to hide. But on no account must he express curiosity, a quickening of the cardiac tempo, naked fear or blind lust. On no account must he feel that he is in the City's heart, an organ which is complex, palpitating with incessant activity and filled with assorted ventricles, tubes, valves and chambers. Behind those leprous medieval façades and bulging timber frames rotting slowly through the centuries he must imagine masochistic circuses and sad little dramas of incontinence and relief such as are appropriate to the subdued and fraudulent sexualities of bald septuagenarians in crinkled raincoats and hordes of industrial managers from the Ruhr in white shoes and rhinoceros-skin belts.

Oh, how superior you feel here, how permeated with luminous and omniscient perceptions, how above it all you are, how astrally inclined, how desexualized, how contemptuous and politically subversive! What a little Engels you suddenly become, confronted with all this social and sexual misery! Not for you these pathetic displays of prostitution; not for you all this crass genital tourism. After all, in the City of Light, you have better things to do and more enlightened ways to spend your evenings than patrolling up and down a half-lit street half a kilometre long in the company of such hideous types, leering lechers, bunny-rabbit women swathed in cuddly fur, bored cops and the endless stream of white-clad

Nordic visitors. What could be more sad, dismal or dangerous?

Our peasant, however, is not of the same opinion. He spends
a truly inordinate amount of his free time patrolling the rue St
Denis in just this way and not for a minute is he dissuaded
from doing so by the thought that one of his cultured and
disapproving friends, passing through perhaps safely ensconced
in a car (those cars that crawl at the slowest possible speed down
the street manned by drivers who can hardly keep their eyes on
the road), might accidentally catch sight of him chatting to one
of the hookers . . . perhaps – what could be more excruciatingly
embarrassing! – the twenty-stone mama from Zaire at the corner
of rue d'Aboukir or the giant blonde sabre-toothed tiger loitering
around the end of the rue Blondel baring her teeth at the terrified
and puny male specimens edging their way nervously around
her. What shame and consternation! What universal condemna-
tion! The rows of beady eyes . . . the accusing looks . . . the
knowing winks. But we might as well come clean: our hero
is an addict and that's that. Neither chains nor fire could keep
him away. He has to have his fix, even if it is only in the form
of an evening's voyeurism. And, in addition, it should not be
forgotten that this fertile thoroughfare is not just a sexual bazaar:
sweat-shops, secret and graceful covered arcades, the passages
that remind us of the sub-vitreous shopping malls which once
ran from one end of Paris to the other in the nineteenth century,
swarming boutiques and its proximity to the *pêle-mêle* of the
garment district make the zone an ant-hill of relentless activity,
a restless nest of termites where the human density is suffocating
and intense.

Athough at certain times of the week the street can suddenly
empty itself and revert to its rustic quiet, there are times, in
the heat of summer, when the ancient world comes alive again
between the triumphal arch of St Denis and the rue de Turbigo.
Chains, chinchilla, *brocatelle* and stockings, leather straps and
studs, nightshade lipsticks, SS boots, body-nets, gladiator belts,
stillettos, leopard skins, matador hats, beryl earrings, watered
silk elbow gloves, French Resistance outfits, the Girl Next
Door outfits, Your Worst Nightmare-Fantasy outfits, Bat from
Hell outfits, I'm Waiting for My Favourite Bullfighter outfits,

Wouldn't You Like to Squash Me outfits, Snow Queen outfits, Wicked Fairy outfits, Naked Savage outfits, You Tarzan outfits, Be Sweet, Gentle but Naughty outfits, Eat Raspberries off My Tongue outfits, Inca Princess outfits, Blue Angel outfits, Let Me Suck Your Neck outfits . . . how can you remain so cold and aloof? Do you mean to say that none of this interests you in the slightest? All the races of mankind are present here, from Eskimos to Melanesians and every fantasy is ticking over somewhere in the dark, and you stand by with your hands in your pockets wondering why it is allowed? The spangles and G-strings drift in front of you . . . you are in a sea of opium, the pungent opium of paid sex. Why not recline like the pasha you have suddenly become and float in the current of sexism? Mashers of the world, unite! You have nothing to lose, after all, but your erections.

A few years ago, during a turbulent summer, the peasant rented a flat on the top floor of no. 265 at the Strasbourg-St Denis end of the street. The large building has a courtyard lined on one side with tall mirrors belonging to the Ateliers Sandra clothes shop on the ground floor. Over the impressive doorway a stone ogre gapes flanked by sculpted pine-cones and the usual twisted laurel leaves. The apartment is surrounded on all sides by rooms rented to prostitutes and gives on to another court on the inner side, at the bottom of which is the glass roof of a textile factory. Through the missing panes of glass in this roof can be seen rows of Pakistani faces sweating over sewing machines and racks of multi-coloured coats. Opposite, dozens of windows arrayed below the skyline, a forest of aerials and, far away, the dome of the Opéra. In these endless lines of windows can be seen the pullulating dramas which are played out under the aegis of St Denis. At every landing window, a pimp idling away empty hours, and in the adjacent windows, always empty in the stagnant heat of summer, the peeling walls of the love-nests. Projected against them, flashes of naked bodies, the flicker of money and the odd bra tossed in the air.

While brushing his teeth by his bathroom window, for example, our impressionable hero was confronted, in the flat just opposite, with the daily sight of a small shabby bed next to which, carefully plugged in at the wall, reposed two giant electric dildos in a metal box. Below this room nothing could be seen except the continuous exercising of a pair of brown thighs clasped frantically around pairs of white bouncing buttocks. But usually only the feet were visible and so the casual spectator-voyeur was treated to a tango of red high heels and white brogues danced according to rigid rules of engagement, never missing a step or skipping a heart-beat. The dizzying speed of these multiple consummations, all taking place simultaneously as on a hundred different television screens, called for a certain agility of the eye and brain. A hundred copulations a minute! Multiplied by a hundred down the length of the street . . . a staggering calculation! Nor did the dances stop for a minute, from eight in the morning to eight. Millions, no, tens of millions of feet dancing the tango of sex, millions of times a year. What an industry worthy of the Age of Efficiency, more impressive even than the building of the Great Wall of China. He could not stop himself trying to imagine, in the most vulgar and horrific way, the sheer quantity of semen being expended every week. Enough to multiply the population of the globe by ten. And enough money to buy Paraguay.

The various comings and goings of the three or four blocks assembled around this large interior space were governed, however, by secret forces that only occasionally showed their faces to reveal where all this money was destined. One night a pimp was murdered at the bottom of the stairs opposite, knifed by the Tong, pandemonium exploded on the staircases and a flock of Arab girls came crashing down them screaming 'Les jaunes! Les jaunes!' Was it the Tong who were rumoured to control the building, the prostitutes and the drugs they used, or does the fantasizing intelligence of the dumb witness like to jump to such conclusions? There is no reason it should not have been a hired Tong killer, for shortly afterwards our peasant certainly heard an intruder beating up a street girl in the flat next to his . . . slaps, shouting, incriminations, and then the sound of a television set hurled from the window crashing into the glass roof five storeys below followed by its owner, who was found in several pieces among the spangled coats, apparently with fingerprints all over her. They say that a Tong man will kill any casual or accidental witness and so it was not prudent to lean out of the window too far and observe what was going on. But the thought of Chinese hit-men armed with machetes and .38s fitted with silencers creeping through the warren of rooms regulating everything from behind the scenes is too irresistible for our peasant, weaned as he has been on *films noirs* and the adventures of Fantômas so closely fitted into the Parisian landscape. In any case, the duels that are fought behind the façades of the rue St Denis are in no way inferior in violence and exoticism to the marginal brutalities of mythic cities of twenteith-century crime elsewhere, only it is a violence that is discreet, unnoticed and hallucinatory. The day after the body and the television set hit the roof, the glass had been swept away, the sweat-shop was back to normal and nothing was mentioned in any newspaper if not the usual single sentence under a cryptic small headline on page eighteen. No other city sweeps its crumbs so swiftly under the carefully brushed carpet.

During his months here, however, the peasant gradually acclimatized himself until even the feminine Gestapo thugs hanging about in his doorway called him by his first name and it was then that he became a self-taught expert in the system of prostitution, the rules, regulations and nuances of which must be carefully observed if transactions with the denizens of St Denis are to pass off smoothly and normally.

The rue St Denis extends from the Porte St Denis by the Strasbourg-St Denis Metro station as far as the rue de Rivoli near the Place du Châtelet, but it is only the stretch from the Porte to the junction of the rue de Turbigo and the rue Etienne Marcel that is given over to prostitution proper. This red-light zone also includes the several side streets, passageways and alleys that subtend to the rue St Denis itself.

On certain nights, a vast congestion of heaving heads, torsos, thighs and mouths blocks the main street and the alleys, the rue Blondel, the Passage Basfour and the junction of rue Réaumur, where the run of sex shops begins. In the Passage Basfour, in the southern half, shattered old tarts pose in the half-darkness on the saddles of motorbikes and in the rue Blondel, in the northern half, half-naked atrapas in beaver coats stand against the walls of the tiny street all night, as white or Asiatically light-tinted as the Ghanaians of the parallel rue Ste Apolline are blue.

In the city of the future, the spatial organization of pleasure will be far more convenient than today's random and chancy gambles. Instead of playing with the possibility that in descending Blondel at two in the morning the imperious male perambulist, feeling dangerous swellings in his *corpus spongiosum*, might just find the cute Eurasian in leather jodhpurs who hangs around the Escale bar, but then again might not, the masher of the future will have at his disposal a system derived from the highly moral English example of grovellingly euphemistic newsagent ads. Of course, those oblique notices pasted in the windows by desperate night nurses and unemployed 'school mistresses' desperate to exert a bit of gratifying discipline will have to be replaced with something a little more appetizing. After all, the English *tone* in these matters is anything but appealing. No, the Paris masher of Futuropolis will want it full in the face, no punches withheld. Obeying future laws that will nevertheless govern the propriety of the streets (yet again following the noble British example of urban antisepsis), the customer will find along the walls of the rue Blondel or the rue du Ponceau not the hordes of beautiful and exotic sex slaves he sees there today but rows of video installations which – rather like the information screens in the Les Halles underground complex – will provide reams of searing information at the mere touch of a finger. Vital statistics, date of birth, racial composition, blood group, medical history and certificates, relevant vaccination record, full colour photographs of all bodily parts and even clips of explicit films which will show the wonder-struck john just what his prize-to-be looks like on the job – all will flash before his eyes on the screen as he selects each section with his index finger. Not only that, but the sound of the woman's voice, listing her prices in a happy and convivial tone, will be activated by the simple push of a button. In short, it will have been understood once and for all that the object of what is now called prostitution (but which in the future will go by more pleasant names – 'empathetic release procedures', 'physical reciprocity procurement', 'love–finance systems') is to remove, without fear of retaliation or sudden moral exposure, the mystical element of chance that governs the obtaining of sexual gratifications. Even the faintest possibility of female refusal or frigidity is categorically removed. Possession is instantaneous.

It is a commercial idea of genius, attributable, so they say, to the cynical but alluring priestesses of Ur who . . . but the priestesses of Ur will be non-existent to the masher of the future who, strolling lecherously down the babbling rue Blondel, will have only the future on his mind and who, in addition, will have instantaneous possession in its most perfected form. Push a button and there she is, with a pink computer-coded receipt between her teeth and a magnetic tape stuck to her buttocks. You will be able to choose her clothes, her make up, her smell, her underwear; you will stick your bank card into her socket and watch your time expire on a digital clock carved into her neck.

How, then, will it be possible to imagine the open-air barless cages of today when they have disappeared? They will be as remote as the 100,000 girls of the *fin de siècle* participating in the golden age of whoredom. And how is it possible to imagine that age, the age of Cora Pearl and Mademoiselle Maximum, the glorious epoch of the courtesan chronicled in the fantastical pages of Arsène Houssaye and that strange and obscure historian, 'Zed'? The vampire-whore of the Second Empire, with her block shares in Royal Dutch and Transoccidental Spices and her spectacular *imbroglios* hatched in the infamous Room 16 of the Café Anglais, her wad of calling cards from the collective membership of the Jockey Club and the footloose aristocrats of the Age of Pleasure, the Grammont-Caderousses and Ducs de Morny . . . she is as unimaginable today as the hysterical black heroines of Shakespeare or the Didos of rococo ceilings. There is no means of associating the sexual remnants of the tradition of the 'grandes horizontales' who loiter in the network of St Denis alleys, the purple Pigalle bars with open windows and the indexes of contemporary dating agencies with the *filles de joie* of that lost century. The open air gardens of the Bal Mabille with their hanging lamps and promiscuous shaded *promenoirs* are as unimaginable as the 'revues' of the Marquis de Massa. The political and financial power of the prostitute has evaporated, along with her cultural prestige, sealed by the opulent portraits and group pieces of Meissonier and Alfred Stevens. Regardless of factual knowledge of the empire of syphilis and the secret history of spirogyra that underlies it, the age of the courtesan succeeds in imposing its atmosphere of nostalgia and romance, the meteoric lives of the cocottes – Otéro winning thousands at the Monte Carlo casino at the age of thirteen, Léonide Leblanc burning thaler notes as Maryland cigarettes at the galas of Baden-Baden, Paiva demanding that Adolphe Gaiffe burn thousand-franc notes for the duration of his passage through her *lit d'apparat* – will never be repeated, just as their props, the *bouchon de carafe* diamonds, the Duleep Singhs and upholstered broughams, have become as unthinkable as the possibility of thoughtful life on Uranus. From the social apogee of Chrystianne de Chatou's Inca Ball held at the courtesan's house on the rue Fortuny in the year 1900, for which Massenet composed what is now the national anthem of El Salvador, the prostitute has subsided to the figures of the rue Blondel, pastiches of air stewardesses, lion tamers, schoolgirls and the mythic courtesans themselves. The prostitute for the first time is in danger of becoming a pastiche of herself. She no longer belongs: she is doomed to ever-accelerating convenience. She is on her way to the video screens of the ideal future.

In the glare of day the rue St Denis is crossed and re-crossed millions of times an hour by the hordes of ephemeral Pakistani and Indian porters hired by the garment district, who whiz and weave their way through the maze of parked cars, matted pedestrians and tarts, with their small steel trolleys and two-wheel lifters piled high with enormous packages or whole clothes racks on castors laden with astrakhan coats or embroidered pyjamas. The covered arcades come alive and the whores take a back seat. In the doorways of the boutiques immaculately turned-out managers and salesgirls stand sur-veying the influx of their wealth, a small-scale flow of cash, perhaps, but intense and pregnant with kitsch nevertheless. In the innumerable courtyards and functional passageways that open up on either side of the street sewing machines hum, needles click and tiny warehouses clatter with frenetic deliveries. The richest and most important thoroughfare of medieval Paris relives in echoes the forgotten glories of its silk merchants, milliners, goldsmiths, bankers and tailors, those proud and prosperous merchants capable of covering the street with a 'sky' of silk sheets during the progress of the monarch on his way to Notre-Dame and who, during the said procession of

Louis XI following his coronation in 1461, were able to fill the street's four public fountains with milk, wine and hippocras. The rue St Denis remained a district of luxury boutiques, despite the departure of many firms during the Fronde for the rue St Honoré, until well into the nineteenth century. Perceiving the efficacy of the St Denis barricades during the revolution of 1830 Napoleon III decided to pierce the *quartier* with the large Boulevard de Sébastopol, opened in 1858, so initiating the rapid decline of the rue St Denis. Thenceforth the most popular term of indignation used by the preachers of the last century and a half when describing the honeycomb of streets has been 'vile cloacas', a term just and blind in equal measure. For St Denis, preserving its medieval fabric against all assaults, still harbours the ghosts of its past heroes and the enigmas of its lost prestige. Is it not significant that the street of the fourteenth-century metropolis so closely associated with pilgrimage, religious hospitals and secluded devotion should have become the 'cloaca of vice' of the present City? The rue Blondel itself, formerly the rue des Deux Portes, formed one side of the convent of the Filles de l'Union Chrétienne. The Passage du Trinité, most typically cloacal of all the cloacas, was once part of the site of the Hospital of Saint Trinité, the vast thirteenth-century sanctuary, harbour of pilgrims and the sick and model of generous piety and social responsibility. At no. 237 stood the sanctuary of the Filles-Dieu, where the condemned had the right to kiss a cross and be served bread and wine before being hanged at the Montfaucon gibbet, for along with the procession of kings the rue St Denis accommodated the final procession of criminals on their way to the City's principal places of execution and humiliation, the pillory at Les Halles and the sinister Montfaucon. Thus the street appropriately guards the memories of Henri de Taperel, who argued his way with the crowd all the way down the street in 1320 on his way to death at Montfaucon and of the eleven felons sentenced to decapitation at Les Halles in 1430, one of whom was pardoned due to the moving protestations of love of a young girl living in the street.

During the Mardi Gras the Porte St Denis was the point of entry for the King of Fools equipped with his ass's ears, and the grotesque imagery carried by the merchants' guilds during the royal processions, effigies of the seven deadly sins, has lingered on in the cloaca, where nothing has been randomly torn down. The rue St Denis itself passed by the Innocents' cemetery before it became the Place des Innocents after the removal of the human remains to the catacombs in the 1780s, and here, painted on one of the walls of the galleries, was Europe's oldest fresco of the Dance of Death, now vanished along with the formidable necropolis that housed it. For centuries this lower end of the street was suffused with the sweet and nauseous odour of ptomaine, the gases released by millions of corpses, and the odour of necrophilia has never been quite submerged by the street's subsequent evolution. Dank and ferocious memories are rarely far from its material surface, deposited there by the violent twitches and spasms of history as much as by the memory of communal burial ditches. At 23 rue Beauregard, a stone's throw from the thoroughfare, lived Catherine Deshayes, the practitioner of black magic and infanticide burned alive in 1679 for the murder of 250 new-born children subsequently buried in her back garden: a presence as phantomic as that of Renée de Vendômais, walled up alive by the Innocents in 1486 for complicity in the murder of her husband. More angelically, the ascetic Alix la Borgotte had herself walled in voluntarily at the same place in 1420 and died peacefully forty-six years later in 1466. A gap in the texture of medieval houses at the corner with the rue des Lombards marks the place where the Huguenot Gastines were burned alive in front of their house, which was then destroyed. And it was near here, from his tower on the rue Etienne Marcel, that the brutal Jean sans Peur, the Duc de Boulogne, launched his finely planned assassinations before being murdered himself in 1419. And isn't the reign of magic and sorcery announced by the enigmatic astrological tower on the near-by rue de Viarmes erected by Catherine de Médicis in 1572 and at the top of which her astrologer, Ruggieri, used to discourse with the stars?

The arcades are the last optimistic architecture to have been added to the dense patchwork of the former merchants' quarter. The Passage du Grand Cerf was covered over with glass in 1825 after the closure of the great hostelry of the Grand Cerf and today it is closed altogether while awaiting reconstruction, its elaborate pediment over the entrance – characteristic of the shy bombast that announces all these arcades – and fanciful vaults slumbering in an inaccessible solitude and darkness. But its sister, the Passage du Bourg l'Abbé across the street, is functioning, though in a twilight world of its own. The glass barrel vaulting, supported by wooden pilasters covered with rusted grilles, lets a light without moods fall down among the dull clothing shops with, in their windows, the latest fashions from Bucharest. The passage is filled with these Eastern European boutiques until the shopper emerges at the other end of the rue de Palestro where, without warning, a gate of overblown magnificence awaits him, a shining example of industrial Grecian consisting of two gigantic caryatids on either side of the grille gates shining with gold spikes, each one provided with sturdy symbols of heroic industry – an anchor, a winch, an anvil. Clearly our ancestors were infatuated with the world of labour. In this passage it must once have been possible to find in close proximity to each other exotic tea merchants, ticket offices for passages to the gold mines of Brazil, vendors of spades and nautical clocks and mezzanines filled with shipping clerks and millionaire sugar traders. Perhaps it was even as hot as the tropics inside and dazzling with colonial splendour. In any case, retracing his steps, the nostalgic shopper sees, as a lonely memento of that distant epoch of leisure, only a faded monochrome enlarged photo of a yacht anchored in what looks like the Baie des Anges propped up inside a veiled shop window. If the Bourg l'Abbé was once awake and alert it is now immersed in its own sleep, a sleep that will probably end in slow decomposition. But should anyone suddenly be tempted to read into this prophetic moralisms concerning the Death of the City it will only be necessary to follow our advice and make your way to the next arcade up, the Passage du Caire, the largest of the covered arcades and the one most infused with the insectal commercialism of the garment industry. The cloaca of St Denis – and these claustrophobic bazaars are reminiscent of the Cloaca Maxima of ancient Rome, the world's oldest sewage pipe – are only partially asleep. And if it comes down to it, is it not the City's capacity to sleep that is its most alarming and interesting characteristic? The inability to sleep is what makes the world's

Futuropolises so nightmarish and the sleeping parts of Paris are the parts that most appeal to all true peasants. Unfortunately, the magnificent Passage du Caire is hardly ever asleep, except when it is locked up for the night. On principle, this strange tunnel should be open to the public at night, when its dreamlike atmosphere might finally be appreciated . . .

The Passage connects the rue St Denis and the relaxed Place du Caire, that oasis of burlesque Egyptiana. The glass roofs are pyramidal and strangled by an undergrowth of pipes, wires and assorted tubes all encrusted in a film of black fluff. Attempting, probably, to recreate the underground nuances of a Cairo bazaar, it bifurcates at several places to form a system of passageways which are punctuated from time to time by the charming blue hanging lamps of the few *concierges* who still reside here. Strings of coloured bulbs cross the air above the endless parade of utilitarian stores, mostly fabric wholesalers, window decorators and domestic hardware outlets. By the Sapon store the main alley divides and the right-hand path leads off to eventual union with the rue d'Alexandrie and its desultory square fringed by sweat-shops and warehouses. The principal artery continues directly to the Place du Caire, opening up minor tributaries on the way, most of which run down to the parallel rue du Caire. Our hero is filled with curious relief when emerging into this little-known triangular square populated by casual knots of Pakistanis, freelance porters and the local traders, who congregate in the café adjoining the entrance to the arcade. This entrance is flanked by Egyptian columns with acanthus capitals and above it rises one of the most extraordinary structures in the City, a colossal statement of architectural pastiche which is routinely ignored by everyone in the square. In the middle of the structure are fixed to the wall three gigantic Nilotic heads with the crinkled ears of baby elephants and with box-shaped sacramental head-dresses. Their sloping eyes are elongated to the point of farce, caricature of an extinct race. The acanthus columns extend into the room of the café itself and above, on the two top floors, they are echoed by arcades of palm-leaf columns inset into the wall. Above these runs a jutting eave laboriously inscribed with vague Egyptian motifs copied arbitrarily from a museum exhibit: a duck eating a serpent, an eagle, a monkey, a falcon and then, bizarrely, a human profile surmounted by a fez and provided with a nose as big as a cauliflower. Below him, in a centre frieze of bas reliefs, runs a comic strip of war chariots, tethered slaves and triumphant kings. Slender columns blinding the vertical edges of the building are made to imitate, by means of criss-crossing lines, long bundles of papyrus. And over the entrance to the passage sits a double-headed cobra with magical outstretched wings announcing, by implication, the eruption of the esoteric.

This bogus imagery dominates the Place du Caire for the same reason that an Egyptian pyramid dominates the reverse side of a dollar bill. The spirit of orientalism runs through the history of the City like the frequent bouts of disorientation suffered, or rather enjoyed, by the lifelong opium addict. Its fantasies throw up curious products. The New Age credo that a pyramid-shaped kennel keeps Fido cosmically attuned is intimately related to the Masonic lucubrations and their derivatives which stress the importance of the Egyptian contributions (thousands of years before our own time, of course) to space travel and intravenous medicine. No matter where you walk in Paris you will find fragments of Egyptian paraphernalia. You are walking, for example, down a perfectly normal street when, lo and behold, there is a sphinx sitting on top of a garage wall or a bust of Amenhotep II peering at you from a gatepost, faces blank, purposeless and crumbled, evidence of a universal desire to transcend the present. The rue Férou by the Place St Sulpice is not only typical in this respect, it is almost foreseeable. The formidable tradition of mental lust for the anti-Occidental, the inexhaustible spirit of chinoiserie, has never loosened its hold since it was let loose among the intellectuals of the eighteenth century, though these Egyptian reveries in stones are the most anodyne and innocent of its expressions. A monstrous eclecticism lingers in the metropolitan air, happily continuous with the indescribably barbaric pavilions of the Great Exhibitions of the last century, in which whole Amazonian villages, Moghul lavatories, Ming bathrooms, Malaysian mosques and Kirghiz yurts, the Green Mosque of Bursa and Roman catacombs were reproduced with minute accuracy down to the last detail. A quixotic vulgarity that makes itself forgivable by its occasional sheepishness. The Place du Caire keeps its treasures to itself while remaining the axis of Cairo-in-Paris. And yet a few steps along the rue du Caire are enough to put it entirely behind you, and once you have regained the rue St Denis it dissolves into the chaos that reigns in your frontal lobes and disappears without trace. Soon this entire district will follow it into nothingness, for such a large zone of the fantastic seems predestined perpetually to modify itself.

There is only one more passage that deserves description, if we exclude the solemn and graceful Passage du Ponceau, which is classical and domestic: the Passage du Prado on the Boulevard St Denis, where strange pale-grey vaults sport inset mirrors and orange penis-shaped columns . . . abstruse insignia of vanished cults. Of all the covered arcades, it is the most recalcitrant, the most eccentric. Its L shape is joined at the angle by means of a large glass dome and an eerie circular square beneath it. In this lost burrow of the City the Hotel du Prado resides in all its enigma, a curving glass window of a reception area giving on to the square, blank and dark. To its right is a workshop with the familiar whine of sewing machines – three Pakistanis labouring over piles of cloth, posters of the Himalayas on the wall and Pasha tour guides to eastern Turkey, and Frank Sinatra blaring out from somewhere deeper within. The long bulbs fixed to the octopus frame of the dome are occasionally lit and turn the scene into something more fairyish. The rue St Denis once flowed with lace and handkerchieves. Madeleine Clergease, the handkerchief-maker, was its patron saint. It flowed with gold and copper, and Guillaume Desaufiers was its guardian angel. Today there are the Pakistanis and their obsolete Singer machines, pantyhose production lines, seas of panties and nylon bras, thermal underwear and string vests, tweed trilbies and polyester ties, sweat-absorbent soles and plastic shoes to go with them. In the process of becoming a cloaca, the royal thoroughfare has made the vertiginous descent from gowns of silk to disposable raincoats with synthetic linings. The 'skies' of satin have turned into a forest of vertical plastic signs and the lines of spacious, accommodating shops transformed into the crannies of the honeycomb, the pockets of space where there is a frenzied, maddening crepitation of insects . . . the buzzing of anthropomorphic bees. And like bees they are busy copulating, hoarding, running, dancing, carrying, flying, working and copulating again. The cloaca of Paris are filled with the miraculous industry of bees . . . and in the Passage du Prado, as in all the 'underground' arcades which are the best mementoes of a violated past, the spirit of the hive is alive, the world of the insect is alert.

A peasant's head is always full of memories . . . the highway of whores fills him with involuntary reminiscence.

> *putas*
> *pilares de la noche vana*

The Mexican poet is not describing Paris, nor even Mexico City, he is observing the eternal return at the crux of the flesh trade. It is a hot summer evening and the peasant approaches an Arab girl by the grocery store of the rue Greneta. There is nothing attractive about her, nothing extraordinary. She is dressed in a fluffy white woolly cardigan and black dress. The light fails and turns green as they cross the street and mount the stairs. There is an excruciating queue outside the rented room, muffled sounds, sly grins all round, the Algerian pimp shaking everyone's hand. Almost like a family picnic, sympathetic and informal. It seems that the girl is Berber, not Arab. She hardly speaks a word of French. Their discussion slides into absurdity. She tried to name figures, throws up fingers. Her face is shaped like a strange crystal, bulging at the sides, and in the middle of her forehead (it is this which no doubt attracted him to her) is a paling blue tattoo. She is naïve and nervous. Her teeth are black at the edges, he remembers those teeth from the Sahara. Finally the door opens and out steps a lithe and charming tart with a radiant smile. Behind her, clumsy, awkwardly self-conscious, a fat fellow with straggling hair slipping across his face, stuck down with sweat. It's been a heavy session. He looks devastated. Her purse is bulging with notes. So he went the whole way, 500 francs! Through some desire to please, the Algerian ushers in the Berber girl and the peasant and they find themselves alone. An awkward moment.

He opens up conversation and she throws up the same fingers. But at the same time they smile at each other. There is resignation in the air. She undresses slowly, takes off her tights, looks over at his body with curiosity, her own is coffee-brown, fragile and thin except around the hips, the slender beauty of the desert. He touches her arms. They are breakable. She doesn't know what to say, although it is clear she wants to say something. They sit side by side on the bed – a ridiculous gesture. They can't stop smiling. For once, there is nothing uneasy in the movements, the room is warm and well decorated, a far cry from the cubicles on the rue de Budapest equipped only with a candle and box of tissues. What is happening? The blue tattoo . . . it seems to smudge under the trickles of sweat appearing on her forehead. And suddenly he sees what it is about the tattoo. It's in the shape of the Cross of Lorraine, the symbol of the old Action Française or the Free French, he can't remember, in any case a potent symbol of national purity. The Cross of Holy France is emblazoned in her forehead and trembling under its pool of sweat. She turns her face sideways. She says something in her Berber dialect. Perhaps she would like him for a husband. Her working papers are stuffed carelessly into her wallet, along with his money. Is she smiling about that? Her lips are covered with faded rose lipstick clumsily applied and her teeth peep out when she smiles, hideous and irregular, black at the crown, brownish at the root. And yet he likes her teeth as much as her Cross of Lorraine tattoo, they are suffused with the same gentleness and absence of calculation. The almost-black aureoles of her breasts are the same colour as the rotted crowns of her teeth. It is perfect, everything tied up into a quiet whole. She could be dreaming about the oases of the Draa. She could be dreaming about castration. She could be dreaming about retirement.

They take a long time and there is a tap on the little door. They help each other dress. Small intimacies, like a married couple! At last the door is opened. She hangs back, waiting for him to go out first. No, he wants her to go out first. She doesn't understand. It's politeness, he insinuates. You're the man, she insinuates back. A small fiasco ensues. Neither of them moves. It is imperative, after their wholly unexpected interlude of tenderness, that a wholesome etiquette be observed. In the end, seeing her absolute refusal to be impolite or to fail to do what a woman is expected to do, he grabs her by the shoulders and propels her through the door. But after that there is another door to get out into the hallway and the same thing repeats itself. He pushes her firmly out in front of him. What slaves of form they both are! But at least she is enjoying herself. Yes, she's really quite pleased to be propelled through doorways by her client! She is confused at the same time. And at the final door giving on to the street she resists, through the power of instinct and education, a third time, then, apologizing for no reason, steps through the door of her own accord. It is night, as always. They say goodbye. She invites him to look her up for a drink one of these nights, and she does this miraculously, using just her fingers. It is extraordinary, the power of fingers. She walks off and the moon rises over the rue de Turbigo, inflamed, melon-orange, glacial. Despite all climatical, astrological and metereological declarations to the contrary, it is another white night by St Denis.

Aladdin's Cave

Paris is full of inventive and playful peasants and has always lent itself to the nomadic descriptions of these pseudo-gipsies, posing as poetic rustics, who abuse her generosity, defy her materialism and flaunt their unease in her face. The City possesses a lop-sided momentum that throws them off their feet. Although they are embarrassed to admit it, our legions of literary and artistic peasants are spiritually raped by her excesses, the flow of luxury and money, the reactionary order of her streets, the fabulous stability that plays at revolution and the mysterious delirium of her inhabitants. Full of ignorant but fruitful superstition, they fantasize about the brains behind those Parisian noses, the texture of their mythic food, the aura of violence emanating from the sewers and the Metro and the amazing stream of words that continually flies through the air bouncing off objects and people like the maniacal warbling of millions of birds. The City's material beauty dazzles them because it is intricate and porous, divided into domestic, manageable zones, always adjusted to the human eye, an optical effect of balanced space, horizons secreted only by history or by forgotten and therefore forgivable ideologies, and because it is an astounding anomaly in the galaxy of the world's advanced metropolises. The peasant who happens to arrive from Los Angeles or London is not sure whether it is a gigantic joke designed to fill him with shame. But then, it is not possible to play at being a peasant in other cities. Only in Paris is the explosion of the nightmare megalopolis incomplete.

Some of our fellow peasants are filled with joss-scented fantasies of alternatives to the queen city of Europe: the Islamic City, the Communist City, the Eco-City, the Animal-Liberated City, the Tobacco-Free City, the Anti-Industrial City, the Eastern City, the Zen City or simply the Anti-City City. Let our peasant comrades and partners in holistic medicine be warned, however. The City does not partake of alternatives. It is claimed that, whereas our beloved metropolis is anodyne, inhuman, greedy, exploitative, suffocating, violent, dirty, racist, unspiritual and life-destructive, in other words Western, these other possibilities of the city, actual or imagined, are absolutely and diametrically the opposite, namely, harmonious, whole, spiritual, non-violent, just, pollution-free, arborescent, quiet, kind, ecologically sound, devoid of any kind of exploitation and perfectly in tune with the great and invisible vibrations of the cosmic. They could be called an ascetic poem in stone. The Ideal City is constructed painfully in the peculiar drawing-room of the skull and is filled with gardens, fountains, kindergartens, relaxed mosques and joyfully levitating workers – a soulful fusion of ancient Samarkand and the hygienic amenities of modern Helsinki. But let us confess that the concrete City which we know as Paris was never tuned to the clichés of the afterworld. It has evolved pragmatically and the aroma of its gutters, the cynicism of its grandeur and the alveolate structure of its provincial streets with their humidity and bourgeois industry are a thousand times more alluring than the Celestial City, the City of God or the dead gardens of Samarkand. By dint of a stubborn streak of perversity the City refused to sink into the past. And is it not true that, in imitation of those Eastern metropolises mostly wiped from the face of the earth by the hordes of Genghis Khan, the City has its own fountains distributed throughout its length and breadth, and not just the dark green founts of magical nereids between whose lovely hips the lowest hobo can thrust his mouth to catch the jet of water, but – more fundamental still – the water that flows endlessly down its streets, that surreptitious gutter water that streams across squares, down drains and hills, through sewers and piles of shit, always underfoot and near by, always moving according to the pull of gravity, a water that fills the entire city with a nostalgic and murmuring sound of fountains?

We can state with the utmost innocence and sincerity that if the wily birds of Aristophanes were to descend to earth tomorrow morning and establish an updated ornithic version of the Commune, our peasant would be the first to refuse himself entry to that state of terrestrial bliss and would content himself with the tiny and unhealthy street which, in the years that have passed since that first descent into the Metro, has become his home and from where he can hear the sound of falling water more clearly than anywhere else: the rue André Antoine.

It is here more than anywhere else that the whirlpool of the City finds a stagnant epicentre. The rue André Antoine, connecting the peaceful and picturesque Place des Abbesses at one end and the porno neons of the Place Pigalle at the other, is hardly a street at all. At its top section adjacent to the beginnings of Montmartre, it is only a flight of steps subtending to the Café St Jean and passing along the outer wall of the church of St Jean de Montmarte. At the bottom of these steps, half shadowed by chestnut trees, the peasant lives in a converted theatre whose first-floor window is carved with a head of Bacchus and reclining nymphs. From here, just above the building's iron grille door he can see only the trees, the walls of the church, the flights of steps ascending to the Place des Abbesses and the friendly congregation of Brazilian transvestites sprawling in the corner formed by the building's façade and the angle of the steps. As the street slopes downward, however, following the gradient of the hill, it becomes darker and more uncertain. Swinging to the left it produces a junction by a mysterious white villa and from there offers two possibilities: either a stiff climb up again towards the rue Houdon past blasted tenements whose dripping hallways contain flimsy metal chairs, the faces of African prostitutes and finally, on the left-hand side, the Café Joan; or, on the other hand, a straight stretch of street past windows filled with immigrant washing and a pizza parlour to the Place Pigalle, which blazes red and blue at the end of the dark tunnel.

When he first arrived here there were few streetlights. At night the alley, free of cars, was plunged in darkness. Near the junction there is another small bar, Chez Sylvain, where German tourists are occasionally gunned down for refusing to pay and where the muffled sounds of a knifing are occasionally heard. Down this little river of dark cobbles the water runs on its way from the top of the Butte carrying bits of orange peel, used syringes, cigarette stubs and the odd torn condom discarded by the Brazilians at the top of the street. The graffiti have spread, too, down the steps, as they have everywhere in Paris, the angular imitative scrawls derived from New York subway cars that spell cryptic neologisms and framed letters that suggest the insignia of obscure anarchist bomb squads. The growing sclerosis of the city, its imminent demise, the peasant thinks to himself, because that is how we react to the spread of graffiti, the verbal equivalent of germs . . . and immediately his nostalgia bites. But at least noise has not yet intruded, the street is silent aside from the continual sound of running water. The trees opposite rustle in summer, and nightingales mass in the garden of the church. Above him, on the second floor, the closeted housewife who has not left the mental and spiritual structures of the Occupation, plays her transistor while spitting through an open window, the beautiful woman on the ground floor distorts her amazingly pliable legs into yoga positions on a hexagonal Tibetan meditation table, the former abattoir manager on the third floor double-locks and bolts his door against possible Islamic Jihad attack, while on the fourth the possible perpetrator of such attacks, the severe and moustachioed Yugoslavian Moslem whose two minuscule wives are never seen to leave the building unless it is secretly, at night, by means of tied-together sheets dangled from the top-floor window, shits noisily in a small but scented cabin while intoning verses from the Sacred Book.

On the ground floor, safely withdrawn from the world when it suits his purposes behind a curtain of red and yellow beads behind his door, there is a laxer follower of the True Path, a Tanzanian Ali, *concierge* to the building, whose hidden identity, for those who wish to probe his mysteries, is Aladdin. This can easily be confirmed by entering his single room tucked under the stairs, in the middle of which, amid the paraphernalia of many assumed lives, Arabic dictionaries of medicinal spells, hi-fi equipment, boxes of rabbits' feet, cabinets of tropical oils and herbs, cooking pots scented with clove oil, pots of lemon grass and cardamom pods, dense clothes racks and various firearms, hangs a khaki regulation tropics British army uniform decorated with coloured bands. The elusive and virile Ali, who floats along astral planes at will and who gossips in Swahili with Satan in his dreams, once served in the British army in Burma and was decorated for having killed a Japanese sniper while armed only with a lighted cigarette. In brocaded *barbouches* and trilby he responds to the numerous disturbances at the front door with the circumspection of the jungle fighter, a tiny loaded blue pistol in one hand and a withered

African charm in the other. Invisible in the dark, he pounces upon the thieves and drunks who venture into the vestibule to sleep and deliver his spiritual curses in rapid Swahilo-Arabic. His qualities as Aladdin enable him to perform feats of magic that are the envy of the overweight Portuguese matriarchs who are his competitors. During his long career as British spy, porno star in Athens (the poor black boy seduced by his fat white nymphomaniac employer to the cries of 'No Missee, no!'), judo expert and bodyguard he has perfected his medico-magical skills and there is now no ailment chronic or temporary that cannot be immediately treated by means of discreet patronage of the spirit world.

But these remarkable healing powers have not diminished the aura of black magic that surrounds him and, in addition, the André Antoine Self-Preservation Committee, largely staffed by the Portuguese matrons and of which our abattoir manager is the honourable general secretary, has lately had its attention drawn to what in its minutes has been increasingly referred to as olfactory insurrection. It has been distinctly noticeable that, passing the doors of no. 37, a nauseous, insidiously eclectic pan-African concoction of odours can be detected floating or rather loitering with intent in the air and ready, at the least sign of resistance by passers by, to take by storm their nostrils and enter the premises of their brains with narcotic insolence. The exact composition of this gangrenous and mortal odour has not yet been fully ascertained due to the inexperience of the neighbourhood watchdog in the matter of Indian Ocean spices, but it is certain that cinnamon is present, as are cumin seeds, lyophiled bays, nutmeg, the beloved cloves and cardamoms and various esoteric and inedible resins. Since there is no law against the combination of these materials, the Committee's objections to its appearance can only take the form of a disciplined nasal rejection: a passive act of resistance along vaguely Gandhian lines.

'You have to admit,' the ex-meat man says on the stairs, 'they don't have no respect for our nostrils, which is the same as our pride: they put all that shit in it just to get up our noses, if you see what . . . ah, there it is again, smell! Goat's carcasses and hash! Eyeballs and seaweed! One day they'll go too far with their ginger and nutmeg . . . then God help them!'

The meditationist, met on the same stairs in bare feet that reveal the presence of minute red tattoos, is more universalist in outlook: 'It's one more way to God.'

The old lady with the latest headgear for summer 1942: 'The Boches would have cut their tongues out, I remember . . . *verboten! verboten!*'

The Moslem from Nij smelling of freshly cut mint: 'It is only to be regretted that our brother Ali does not partake of his meals at the correct and prescribed times but at hours which are an abomination to our beloved Prophet (blessed be His name) and an injurious slap in the face to all good Believers, who will not forget this significant transgression in the matter of eating gruel. I will have a word with him the next time I see him and, believe me, in the name of the Prophet of the World (blessed be His name) I will raise the point in his presence!'

These violent reactions are understandable in the light of the powerful smells emanating from Aladdin's Cave which, wafting up through the building, penetrate into every corner of every room. The preparation rituals occur every week on a Monday night and last well into the small hours, at which time chants, the rattling of beads and the soft blowing of whistles can be heard. The boiling pot in the middle of the cave can even be glimpsed the next morning with the odd feather clinging to its rim and the master of ceremonies will appear bleary-eyed and only half alive. When he invites the tenants in for lemon grass and gunpowder tea they see that the ends of his fingers are stained orange and that the pot is full of dark liquid.

'Last night,' he explains in all innocence, 'I had a good session with my Guardian Angel. The stars are in fine positions. Mars is not too strong and the wind is blowing from the direction of Africa. All is well.'

The cave tinkles with gewgaws. A local stillness reigns within it, the silence of a cheap alarm clock and the whisper of the neolithic past combined with the models of the Arab astronomers. It is the summing up and the warehouse of an uprooted life – a little corner of lost Zanzibar in the exploding City. Encyclopedias of astrology, a British army pension book, photographs of seven children, the Japanese audio equipment and a kettle filled with dried African grass . . . but Aladdin, able to fly through space on the backs of genies and transport whole palaces from Basra to Fez, is a being who lives in another world. No wonder there is always a demented and indulgent smile on his face. When the other Ali, the ascetic from Nij, descends to upbraid him, the two sides of Islam, Aladdin and Khomeini, confront each other.

'I have come to discourse with you, brother, on the scandal of your cooking times.'

'Last night was the solstice . . . and my pot has good vibrations!'

'The Leader of the Faithful has written . . .'

'Leave alone, man. I never fucked goats.'

'Are you refusing to discourse? I shall relay this information to the Brotherhood of Pan-Islamic Nationhood this very evening. Do you realize you could be beheaded?'

'Only if Venus is in the ascendant. My Guardian Angel . . .'

'Death, brother, to the debauchees of the City of War. You will have a fair trial, however, and you will confess freely.'

'Smoke?'

The Ali from upstairs smiles condescendingly and starts to climb back up the stairs. In reality, the stench from the room is about to make him vomit. He feels faint and clutches the banister. The small white hat on his head vibrates with alarm and he mutters an appropriate curse before taking out a sprig of mint from his pocket and pushing it into his mouth. The man from Zanzibar knows that he is invulnerable, that the spirits are on his side and that the Prophet (blessed be His name) would always understand a few useful deviations.

In this way the various and only partly indigenous population of no. 37 lives on safely under the tutelage of its guardian spirit and it is noticeable that they enjoy more regular and deeper sleep than any other inhabitants of the rue André Antoine. Only the Brazilians outside, who in any case avail themselves only of the exterior windowsills to have themselves seduced by their mysterious clients, are excluded from the pale of his benevolence. In their jackboots and bobbed platinum wigs setting off puffed creole cheeks, they play games in the street and knock their satin pelvises against the glass door or the ground-floor windows when they are working and occasionally they relay, in a spirit of anti-hetero mischief, Morse code messages to the guardian spirit by means of their three-inch fingernails. The Tanzanian advances with his blue pistol. Insults in bastardized Portuguese follow. The urban jungle! The death of the city! But Ali is not slow to improvise a response. He is not unfamiliar with jungles. He is not alarmed by the cries in the streets, the footsteps of heavy-footed fairies in fishnet tights. They are crying out to their jungle mates, to territorial rivals and all possible biological enemies. *Mierdamierda!* Slowly, taking his time, he opens the front door, dares to peer, squints, takes panicky aim into the dark heart of the jungle and fires.

The Peasant Dreams

Of course, we are aware that the persona of the peasant is not exactly imbued up to the hilt with originality – quite the contrary, dear readers! Those who have done their reading in the literature of Paris will no doubt raise their lips in a contemptuous sneer and point out, with devastating lucidity, historical accuracy and smug Sherlock Holmesian wit that the figure of the peasant is, if anything, clichéd and over-used, that the incomparably greater Restif de la Bretonne and his mercurial heir Aragon have exhausted the vein of the peasant, the possibilities of the peasant perspective on the City, and that any further exploration along those lines is doomed from the start, amounting as it does not only to risible insolence on the part of someone who does not even have the courtesy to be a peasant, but also to the most disgraceful, the most ignoble kind of plagiarism, of copycatism, of non-originality, of derivativeness and just plain lousy stealing! What an uproar!

However, we have an even more shameful confession to make: our desire to express our peasant proclivities comes straight from the heart, it has risen like some bad odour ingenuously, directly from our intestines! We are also seduced in the most naïve way by the idea of peasants. When we indulge in our spurious dreams of the purity of nature and of the lost innocence of the pre-industrial world we do so through the image of the peasant . . . the Angelus, the Pierre Levins chopping corn with the muzhiks, the lonely goatherds of the songs of the Auvergne. We are well aware of the sentimental fraudulence of this procedure, but how else can we represent our confusion, distance and amusement when confronted with the sophistication of Babylon? Besides, it is well known that whereas real peasants are grasping, prosaic, ruthless realists, the displaced, alienated peasant is a dreamer exactly like ourselves. And this reminds us that our own peasant, undoubtedly the biggest dreamer of them all, had a dream the other night that should be related.

It happens that he often lounges by the window with the head of Bacchus and peers out into the street late at night when it is quiet, when the Brazilians have subsided in spirit a little and when the moon has slipped out from between the Parisian clouds. But one night as he is dozing on the sill with the shutters wide open a small and crazy drama materializes in the street under the window. The tall blond transvestite named Barbara is being approached as he stands by the steps waiting for clients by three men dressed in long flowing djellabas and white turbans. The moon that night is gibbous and red and this red light touches their faces under the turbans: with a start of astonishment, the peasant recognizes them instantly as members of the dreaded Hashedeen, the terrorist sect of the great and wily Hassan Sabbah, the twelfth-century Persian guerrilla king whose assassins struck terror into the hearts of believers and infidels alike! After so many centuries, then, they are still alive and well, hiding in the heart of the City and venturing out at night only to execute their sinister sentences! And indeed, they exchange words with the trembling fairy, they reach into their robes and whip out three curved knives which slice into the quivering Brazilian's flesh as quietly as a candle is blown out. The prostitute collapses and the three Assassins immediately begin to daub a message with spray cans along the front of the building. By the time the peasant is in the street, the three long robes are charging down the rue André Antoine towards the boulevard and the Brazilian is dead; on the wall is written: DEATH TO THE CITY OF WAR. Not knowing what he is doing, as if an a dream, the peasant gives pursuit to the Hashedeen, who, being filled with the magical properties of kif, are running as fast as greyhounds.

The city is asleep. Exiting from the rue André Antoine at its bottom end, you are ejected into the Place Pigalle, the circular square with its straggle of telephone booths, news stands, crooners, cafés filled with retired tarts, the all-night Arab bakery and the nostalgic and now dejected fountain at its centre. Here the City never sleeps. Hustlers and cocaine dealers loiter along the raised islands in the middle of the Boulevard de Clichy and the younger, more athletic transvestites (the ones who could seriously be taken for beautiful girls until the last moment) hang around the news stand on the right-hand side of the square and the high-tech automatic toilet from which can be heard a faint trickle of pipelined Mozart. It is three o'clock, the hour when the boulevards here begin to change in character, disgorging unsettled accounts, private hatreds and the vicious business which the light of day will not tolerate. Into this unstable whirlpool of faces and dark forms the Hashedeen plunge, turning left into the Boulevard de Rochechouart and running off in the direction of Barbès. The boulevard rolls up and down like a rollercoaster as it follows the iron vaults of the Metro line eastward, plunging down as far as the station of Barbès-Rochechouart before levelling out on its way to Stalingrad. At night the City's most crowded boulevard is emptied of the millions of ants who swarm the cheap bucket shops in the afternoons that are always hot and only in the centre aisles do desultory knots of Arab adolescents prowl around the all-night neon-lit shooting ranges, dodgem tracks and Wild West peep shows. The Assassins continue to run past the Metro station and finally turn sharp left up the tiny rue Caplat: for at the end of the rue Caplat is the rue de la Goutte d'Or and it is here that the texture of city breaks and permits a hole to appear, a hole which possesses the general features of a suburb of Islamabad or Tehran and whose relation to the City is purely feudal. The peasant follows, but as soon as he does he ceases to be the hunter and becomes the hunted.

The Goutte d'Or, the fabulous rectangle squeezed between the Boulevard de la Chapelle, the Boulevard Barbès, the rue Doudeauville and the rue Marx Dormoy, slides along on a plane of its own, unconstrained by the description of 'ghetto'. Immediately, the uniform flow of imposing stone façades is blown away, plots of orange earth erupt between scrambled fencing and the logic of movement and direction embodied in the City's other streets disintegrates. The little streets veer away from each other, climb and twist, intersect in a quiet and intimate way and veer off again with their cargoes of squawking chickens, underground mosques, African fabric shops and groceries filled with bottles of shampoo. The heart of the zone is the narrow and vertiginous rue Polonceau, where the Faithful come to pray in what looks like a garage with mats and the garbled rue Myrha, transplanted from the back streets of Essaouira, with its poultry butchers serving live

pigeons and cockerels in cages and its volatile *buvette* cafés filled
with the relaxed danger of the unemployed. At its centre lies the
Gothic church of St Bernard, where children, having bounded over
the locked gates, play football in the forecourt in front of flaking
maroon wooden doors covered with graffiti. Behind the church
the winding rue St Luc moves off at a tangent taking its dank open
doorways, dirty cobbles and washing-covered windows with it
and then converges with rues Léon and Cavé – *tagliatelle* alleys
of half-demolished houses, plaster shacks and the same intense
mini-cafés. Café Tlemcen, Café Oran, Café 42, Café Myrha, all
signed with the same letters slapped on with a paint brush and
fermenting inside with the click of backgammon tables and the
scent of kif. In the evenings, the area accelerates its heartbeats,
as the rest of the City does, the grocers come out on to the street
and eat *tajines* on upturned crates, varnished faces from the deserts
of Mauritania, ovular female heads split down the middle with
a single blue tattooed stripe and the spiked heads of beggars in
sand-coloured robes and hoods are disgorged into the flow of the
streets from millions of tiny doorways and with them a stream of
Wolof, Arabic, Turkish, Serbo-Croat and Berber dialects. With
the African women, surmounted by bright red turbans and tied up
with gold and scarlet cummerbunds a foot thick and their tubular
chignons bound up with brilliant canary yellow cloth, come the
hoods in Tabi shoes and bold checks, the Lebanese businessmen
in dented Mercedes, the crumpled suppliants squatting on bits of
cardboard, the Moslem patriarchs threading worry beads through
their fingers, always in the same spot night after night, discharging
hatred at everything around them, and the copper-haired Arab
girls leaning out of windows over lines of laundry.

The evident signs of disintegration and increasing autonomy
which the peasant normally observes around him here give him a
secret pleasure, but it takes only the slightest change in the light for
the harmony of this *quartier* which he sentimentally, in true peasant
fashion, associates with the hive-like interdependence of the ideal
Islamic City to dissolve and turn into the face of vengeance. Under
the moody stars of the City's skies, the suburb of Islamabad can
easily turn the dark blue of ice and secrete the faces of obscure
mullahs, henchmen of the Fedayeen, or simply the face of the
local butcher transformed into a mask so alien that the hand of

the passer by moves instinctively in the direction of a knife which he probably no longer carries. Atavistic racial rivalries erupt in the shadows, the loss of Spain is pitted against that of Constantinople and Jerusalem and green water running through the gutters suddenly shows glints of red. When Aldeberan is in the heavens, the Goutte d'Or glistens like a hunted animal covered with its own blood and mucus. The streets freeze with hatred and then relax again under the pressure of music and hash only to seize up again at the drop of a hat, a clumsy word or one look too many. The micro-city drifts way into space, towards the East or the Land of Saints or towards a pocket of empty space, a vacuum where all its features will intensify and slide into chaos. There is nothing holding it on to the earth. Nothing holds it to the City. It belongs nowhere and could thrive anywhere.

But we have forgotten that we are telling a dream. The peasant has not stopped running from the Hashedeen, who are now, in addition, armed with Uzi machine guns, and the chase has become more desperate, energized by bigotry, fear and religious chauvinism.

He follows them to the tiny Café Ba on the rue de la Goutte d'Or, the original name of which might have been Balthazar before the letters were ripped off. On the wall next to it, incomprehensible to the peasant, is scrawled in Arabic THE CITY OF FAITH. Had he noticed it on his way in, he might have seen, written in the same blue chalk the word GHARB under the blue and white nameplate of the rue Caplat: here begins the West. No sooner, however, does he find himself alone in the street, near the desolate junction of the rue de la Goutte d'Or and the rue de Jessaint with its fountain and half-destroyed houses imprinted with the pink and blue tattoos of ripped-off posters than he knows that he is no longer in the City of War but in that other City, the Dar al-Iman, the Acropolis of Faith. It is too late to retrace his steps or in any other way retreat and from the empty window holes of the blasted building next door that once housed the large Café de la Goutte d'Or the glow of Persian turbans begins to multiply. He knows instantly that he is a dark and malodorous weed in the Garden of Allah and that the long knives of the Fedayeen are after his throat. He runs through the streets saying his Ave Marias, crossing himself again and again, up the rue St Bruno towards the sanctuary of

St Bernard la Chapelle, the last bastion of Christendom in sight, its grey crockets and spirelights defying any muezzin's wail, and so into the rue Affre and up to the church's forlorn façade and neglected forecourt. Do the Crusaders have a patron saint he can pray to? What would the Gothic masons have thought looking down at this pathetic and nightmarish scene? A hundred turbaned heads spawned by the great fortress of Alamut, the Eagles' Nest of the Assassins, come down through the centuries to haunt their descendants! A barbaric and inadmissible idea! Their souls must be turning in their graves. But there is nothing to be done in the realm of concrete fact. The Assassins are everywhere around him and their knives are drawn. Seething with insults, they draw nearer. The sky is red above the outraged spires of the church. Cornered right there by the scrubby little garden and its concrete shelter the peasant sinks to his knees and covers his ears – why? – as the curved blades rain down upon him in unison and in the depths of his hunted brain he can hear, chanted over and over, the words, 'Death to the Dar al-Harb! Death to the reptiles of the City of War!'

He wakes up suddenly just as they are aiming their Uzis to finish him off and immediately feels his ears. They are still there. The City is still humming in the distance, the walls vibrating from the Metro. Bathed in cold sweat, he peers through his bedroom window and sees the Brazilian sitting as usual on the bottom step with a hypodermic needle peeping out of his handbag, powdering his nose in a small round handmirror and humming the songs of São Paulo backstreets. He breathes a sigh of relief. But from then on, whether he likes it or not, he looks over his shoulder as he wanders past the rue Caplat and every day for a month afterwards he searches – though in vain – for the word GHARB written on the wall. And who is to say that the Hashedeen belong only in the realm of educated dreams? Who is to say that the City of Faith has not already erupted within the walls of the City of War?

Paris holds many cities within herself, like the ferocious and ungrateful cubs that slumber in the womb of an old wolf.

The
Boulevard de Clichy

✠

We do not, however, fall in line with the advocates of the Modern Apocalypse (imminent nuclear war, Islamic insurrection or the revolution of the birds). We retch at the mention of Armageddon. If a monotonous obsession with the darker sides of the City is becoming apparent it is only the expression of a naïve, ultra-literary and perverse attraction towards them and the fact that our peasant, for some reason has spent all his life in the City in a state of perpetual poverty that has obliged him to get to know them whether he liked it or not. The area around the rue André Antoine happens to be his kingdom, a domain for which he feels a calm nostalgia and affection: the domain of his first awakening, the backdrop to his increasingly hazardous maturity. The dozy chestnut trees of St Jean de Montmarte are his home, as are all the streets in the square mile around him and above all – if we exclude the maze of Montmartre itself – the Boulevard de Clichy, the red-light zone at the end of his own street whose singular and partly nauseating radiation seeps up all the alleys leading off from it up the gradient of the hill on its north side, and which dominates the lower end of André Antoine with its particularly deranging philosophy.

The Boulevard de Clichy, the most bent of all boulevards, both metaphorically and physically, is not a boulevard like any other: it is a pastiche. Inspiration for Miller-Céline clones, nostalgic with the *cocottes en délire* of syphilitic painters, the birthplace of Oo là là and exposed suspenders, the lonely absinthe and Totor la Terreur, temple of tired sexuality and film-set for La Goulue lookalikes, it sucks into itself from all over Europe a fussing, embarrassing, tittering, semi-inebriated army of tourists whose vast oblong chariots stand around the Place Blanche in an attitude of recumbent and sly aggression. Between the Place Pigalle and the Moulin Rouge neon-and-mirror strip joints in the vague shapes of

85

pairs of opened legs stuffed with esoteric gadgetry send out their demagogic signals across the length and breadth of the two-lane avenue, in the centre of which, on the raised walkway lined on either side with loose gravel, drunks, ambling whores and the resolved dancing girls on their way to the Nashville or Liberty's parade all night, or at least until the first gasp of dawn scatters them with fatigue.

This is his favourite street in the City. He is in the habit of often sitting himself on one of the benches in the aisle, say the one opposite the Bonsai Club, and allowing his mind to become vulnerable to pornographic assaults. The Bonsai itself is a paradigm of what the ultimate *petit-bourgeois* sex palace should look like. With a garish *panache* that would cause riots in a puritan country it visually vomits over the casual passer by, desperately attempting at the same time to provide him with an instant erection by means of its walls of illumined anatomical photos, among which the peasant, sitting on his bench, can see a trio with a black stud, a pair of sapphic twins and a Polynesian nurse in orange stockings. Above, set into a panel of red and yellow neon strips, the giant but pointless word SEXY burns through the night, while beneath it, holding up the entire edifice, are two transparent columns bearing – like withered showcase embryos – two etiolated artificial palm trees. To what do these sinister pseudo-palms refer in the grand empire of lust? Why are our eyes feasted upon such incomprehensible displays? Between them, perhaps, lies the answer, for there is the Japanese hostess in a white leather jacket and fringed cowboy boots, with each of her hieratic breasts pointing to the palms on either side of her. And to her right, magnified by a large mirror, there is a rock garden raised upon a brick dais and there are the bonsai trees, along with an impressive assortment of oriental shrubs, rubber plants, bixias and various strains of climbing ivy. The motif of the Bonsai, then, is vegetation. The customer is re-immersed in the antediluvian jungle that once housed his most infamous and inadmissible desires. On the opposite wall is the gallery of bodies, sections of bodies, ensembles, duos, freaks, performing lesbians and leather fetishists, all blazing in the glory of a vibrant and erotic electric light, all pulsating, as it happens, to the copulatory rhythms of Public Enemy.

A short walk along this middle part of the boulevard reveals a plethora of these magical and sinister palaces, as unreal as those of the Thousand and One Nights. Le Plaisir, the Magic Club, El Ramades, the glorious 'Tahitian club' Vahiné Tahiti, La Nuit with its cheaply atmospheric blue lights, Parret's, the Nashville, the Erotika . . . while in between them, wedged between their montages of gigantic breasts and heaving navels, are the pathetic cafés of the night, the Trois Notes and Aux Noctambules, long, narrow spaces filled with sad old street girls and bruised drifters in crazy wigs, at the end of which can be seen stale crooners and piano players churning out the ballads of despair that have the ring of truth in their eyes and which they listen to all night because they cannot sleep.

But the boulevard is not monolithic, nor are its secrets all wrapped up in fake silver. The peasant relaxes here because the street is actually a maze of intricately combined cells . . . and on the north side it is indented by numerous tiny streets, alleys and enclaves, pockets of urban eccentricity that as often as not go by the romantic names of 'villa' or *cité*: Villa de Guelma, Villa du Midi, Villa des Platanes. An exploration of these submerged and secretive villas reminds the nostalgically inclined that Paris preserves time in a more haunting way than any other city, that the flow of its history leaves behind it indissoluble sediments that linger on in tender vacuums and that have the harrowing effect of graveyards, accusing as they do the present with loss of memory, of forgetting its own obvious fragility and ephemeral mortality. To one side of the restaurant section of the Moulin Rouge, for example, is the gentle Cité Véron, a passageway announced by a blue and white Art Deco sign that might herald unfortunate touristic sentiments, but which in reality discloses a half-somnambulant world populated by the ghosts of the nineteenth-century village it was once part of. The City has surged around it and sealed off its connections but the Cité, like the self-contained catacombs on the Via Appia Antica, has no need of connections with reality. To prove this, a poster on a lonely wall at the end of the alley, stuck to the wall only in yellow morsels, declares the desirability of Universal Revolution and free love above a comical picture of Bakunin. It is signed Spring '67 – but which century? And at the end of the passage, embedded in the little square to one side of the

Renaissance hunting lodge transplanted from the Forêt de Bondy, awaits the fantastical and improbable realm of the old curiosity shop, Ophir.

There are three structures around this silent cobbled court-yard, which is – under certain atmospheric conditions – entirely dreamlike. Facing the alley itself is a curious Gothic villa with curvilinear wooden tracery and crumbling balcony, a delicate fab-rication which houses the Rickx lingerie company. To its left the courtyard becomes more shady and rustic, overgrown by tall and slender trees and filled with the picturesque paraphernalia of the Ophir showroom: a red wagon, ancient tankards, a wooden sign with an arrow pointing to the Chemin de la Cascade, pots of plastic roses, a gigantic pair of bellows. Here the cave of Ophir lurks at right angles to the hunting lodge (a perfect sixteenth-century house in front of which hangs, by an elaborately carved window, an occult lantern on a chain) and through the single, half-screened window can be seen a twilight room filled with the white faces of life-sized puppets. On either side of the door stand two life-sized cardboard Turks with drawn swords and long red robes and to their right a complete guillotine with the blade removed. To the front wall is nailed a bronze lamp-holder of enchained putti half-oxidized and flaking. The Ophir, purveyor of *objets decoratifs*, is filled with alarming and heterogeneous detritus which has a life of its own: the faces of the marionettes smile, the rows of straw hats bask like sleeping cats, the crouching papier-mâché demons and carved wooden masks wink just as the eye alights upon them. At any moment the entire crazy ensemble could easily come to life against the proprietor's will as the local anarchists would no doubt like them to, and the courtyard at the end of the Cité Véron could be turned in a matter of seconds into a zoo of pointless artefacts gibbering and dancing around the trees, unrestrained by the threat of intervention by the riot police and entirely capable of taking the Cité by storm. There are never any faces at the windows here except the make-believe ones. The retrogressive forces of childhood have once more reared their ugly heads and forced the City to skip around and ignore a tiny republic of dreams. And like every republic it is even equipped with its own guillotine.

Further down the boulevard in the direction of Pigalle, the other villas are equally furtive and withdrawn: the Cité du Midi, submerged in the subaqueous light of another age, houses the defunct Pigalle Bains Douches, with their turquoise tiles and burnt-out remains of electric signs and rusted generators clinging like gargoyles to its façade while bundles of sycamore leaves accumulate in the central gutter, and the houses, like abandoned temples of freemasonry, secrete a quiet and abstracted charm. The Villa de Guelma crepitates to the sound of flapping wings and moving water, all others being screened off and subdued as irrelevant. And between the illiterate violet neons of Parret's advertising lesbian floor shows and the desperate Trois Notes is the most secretive and aloof of them all, at no. 60: the Villa des Platanes. This unexpected flourish of Roman baroque recedes back from the boulevard to which it has long ceased to belong behind a massive pair of scrolled iron gates. A cavernous vaulted hall separates the gate from the elongated courtyard at the end of which, distant and hallucinatory, rise a flight of steps and two black Appolonian figures bearing lamps on either side. Plaster bas-reliefs in the hall crowded with rusticated columns throw up the fat faces of pipe-playing monkeys, air-borne cherubim and the swirling pseudo-Grecian garlands that usually accompany lush Alma-Tadema paintings of crowds of vestal virgins languishing around Roman dinner tables with sheepish lust in their eyes. In the Villa des Platanes, we are sure, slavery still exists, gymnastic exercises are obligatory and the sound of operatic orchestras no doubt start up out of nowhere to consummate the inhabitants' love affairs. But next to the sybaritic lights of the boulevards, the fights that break out round it, the doormen of the cabarets forever sticking gilded cards into people's pockets and deliberately standing in their way, its futile elegance is forgotten. The roving eye is more likely to be taken by the Hôtel Rhin et Danube through which a flux of street boys in high heels creates a centre of masculine energy that obliterates all memory of our long-forgotten nooks and crannies.

There's no question that the City is being barbarized, that its intimacy is gradually being ironed out in favour of the creation of an empire of aggression in which the temples of food and sex will soon be as sexless and agastronomic as the cohorts of tourists that use them. When Paris is turned into the world's largest Disneyland, as it will be according to leaked government plans destined to be realized by the year 2000, Clichy will be the site for the ghost train, a mammoth construction project involving six different tracks intersecting in multi-layered tunnels and offering six different forms of horror, all of them resuscitated nightmare memories of the long-dead cities, much as the Middle Ages today are evoked by means of scenes of dungeons and public beheadings. There will be a Transvestite Alley, an Arabtown, an Aidsville, Prostitutionburg, Pedestrian Incubus and Porno Nightmare. The spectators will gasp at the primitive barbarity of their grandfathers and wonder whether things aren't being exaggerated a little for the sake of showbiz . . . the train will scream past the Villa des Platanes and the Cité Véron and the citizens of the twenty-first century will wonder to themselves if human beings could really have lived in such cramped, ridiculous and doubtless malodorous structures none of which, to judge by appearances, was even equipped with satellite dishes or liquid crystal billboards. But then, as the stylish commentator in her smart blue uniform will inform them, in the weird phantasmagoria of history anything is and was possible.

On the far side of the Place Pigalle, in the direction of Rochechouart, experiments are already under way to map out the future functions and physiognomy of the *quartier*. At Christmas, Easter and parts of the summer this stretch of the boulevard comes alive with amusement arcades, strip shows and fortune tellers' caravans which have all the tasteful charm and vitality of downtown Las Vegas, made more authentic and, we could say, humane by a total absence of any real money. Here the joyful itinerant and late-night party-goer will find all that his heart desires and should we not point out to him in passing the especially fragrant allure of the 'Louisiana Blues' strip palace, over whose cardboard façade lusting plantation owners pursue half-naked, giant-breasted slaves in turquoise turbans whose foreheads bear glistening and phantasmagoric drops of sweat – as well as that of the 'Red Harem', where similar scenes are enacted in translucent paint by gibbering eunuchs and swarms of fat beauties with the texture and edible delicacy of onanic pastries? Nor will his aggressive passions of the driving wheel go unsated, for here, at the peak of July, are three separate dodgem tracks, whirlpools of male bravura and crackling poles driven mad by incestuous antagonisms and the audience of teenage girls, who wait like princesses of old to see who will emerge triumphant from the duel of the bumpers and the multi-lingual war of words. Here, in the heat of the summer night, lifted above the menacing dark crowds, baking in the glare of the thousands of 100-watt bulbs, the casual observer can see his local neo-fascist grocer charge across the track in his threatening dark blue chariot, all flashing lights and spitting sparks, and crack broadside into the side of a car bearing three Arab Mujaheddin. He can see the Turkish laundryman from down the street smashing into the Armenian cobbler by the next block down and, almost in the very same moment, the septuagenarian Stalinist from the shoe shop pursuing with howls of derision and flaming white hair in a blazing yellow car the patron of his very own local *boulangerie*, the one who kissed de Gaulle's cheek in the spring of 1945 and whose massive forearms, bushy eyebrows and flour-white lips are sent sprawling by the onslaught of the gleeful but otherwise frustrated and bitter Commie. How many lurking accounts are settled here, how many shameful and private duels are worked out if not into the light of day then at least into the light of the overhead bulbs? How many vendettas find their way into the weaving figures of the laminated cars that bump and squeal into the small hours under the gaze of the 'bread and circuses' masses, who flow from stall to stall ready to shoot at deformed cardboard faces in order to win pink teddy bears and plastic wrist watches, or wander into halls of mirrors where they can see naked pygmies committing obscene acts with pythons, Barbary apes and the odd underwater creature? The existence of these circuses of little cars is an inexhaustible source of tension when the boulevard is filled with the scent of uncontrollable male hormones and the provocation of cheap perfume. Knives are drawn over pride injured in the course of a head-on ramming. Pistols are fired off at random over highly symbolic accidents and clashes on the field of play. But the convenience and multiplicity of the distractions on display, their cheap but effective technology and lascivious naïveté point out the future in large letters. Perhaps the tarot-dealing caravans of Sidi Bouabda and La Source ('a different *arrondissement* every month!') will disappear along with the *brochette* and *merguez* stands and the Seventh Circle peepshow with its female dwarf screaming from within a booth in the shape of an open devil's mouth (its eschatological imagery will be incomprehensible to the children of the next century), but the dodgem principle will surely proliferate.

The immigrant masses will come here in ever greater numbers and play out ever more dizzying fantasies with a handful of coins. The voodoo temples like the one in the Cité Véron, where the curious may step in to take a peep at the throat-slitting of live chickens, will spread as voodoo becomes the nation's, or rather the City's, third official religion and the slaying of various animals on street corners will seem as normal as people hailing taxis there today. Pyrotechnics and fun will progress in synchrony with an upsurge of paganism, confusion and chicken slaughter. The high-speed overhead train on pneumatic wheels will no doubt be fully sound-proofed, so that the wealthy denizens of our curious future will not have to hear the sound that will accompany these amusing and quaint sights, a sound that will be a thousand times more awful than the sound of genocide, such as we may imagine that to be. For the City of the future will be dominated by sound: sound more potent than our dead music, sound as terrifying as nonsense itself, sound as brilliant and lucid as the blade of a guillotine and which will serve more or less the same purpose, namely the chopping off of irritating and inconvenient human heads.

And although the Boulevard de Clichy has not yet reached this interesting pass, it seems to the upstairs Ali, as he promenades alone with or in the company of his radical friends from Skopje and Nij along the central aisle in search of a bit of sly Western fun, that the domain of Satan is indeed not far off in time and that progress is indeed a damned whore and that machines are contrary to the Spirit of God and that one day, if need be, turbaned Luddites will have to smash everything in sight with hammers before a hysterical version of the future becomes real and everything that has gone before, from Allah to Marilyn Monroe, is swept away into the dustbin of history, all faiths together, all words, gestures, methods of baking bread, landscapes, techniques of copulation, ethnic literatures, cuisines, habitudes, etiquettes of hygiene, sacred and unsacred books, modes of transport, working practices, habitual and well-loved tastes, local beauty spots, certain trees, angles of streets, nostalgic streetlamps, hairstyles, footwear, underclothes, perfumes, even our recognizable insects and body odours, all wiped off the face of the earth as if they had never been, scraped from the memory of man, poured like the contents of a litter bin into all the litter bins that have preceded it and leaving nothing behind it but pathetic and humorous scraps, reminders of our utterly forgotten City, idiotic traces of the dead. The dead that live in a black hole called the past. The peasant, too, thinks these thoughts as he sits outside the Bonsai Club, thinking for example of what the skeleton of the white leather geisha will look like when it is accidentally dug up out of a drain in that other black hole that is called the future and what the Bonsai Club will look like in a thousand years' time – for the City is not going to die, being immortal: it is simply going to spit on its past. The evolution of the City is just this continual process of spitting, defiling and trampling underfoot. You are going to be trampled underfoot. The dark room on the rue André Antoine is going to be trampled underfoot, smashed up with spades and drills. The magic cave of Aladdin is going to be turned into a fish pond in someone's back garden, decorated with plastic mermaids; the Villa des Platanes will be buried in earth and over it a giant all-purpose shopping mall will be built called the Platanagora where you will be able to buy soyabean beefsteaks in their millions as easily as the odourless detergent that will gently wash the bowls of your toilets. The future is a tyrant and his boots are covered with blood. And the City of the Future such as it appears in our peasant's lurid dreams, takes the form of that place known to reactionary daydreamers as 'Futuropolis' . . . a new City which is not a dream at all and whose emerging features are already breaking through the surface of the City in order to take its inhabitants by storm. Be prepared, citizens, for earthquakes in the land of the future! Cover your eyes and run for cover! The future is already here, as if you didn't know . . .

Futuropolis

Do not assume, fellow citizens, that our new metropolis will repeat the mistakes of the old: do not assume, either, that it will resemble your most cherished ideas of the future. No, Futuropolis will not be built in the image of classic silent films or of Brave New Worlds, 1984s, *We*'s, Alphavilles or science-fiction techno-nightmares governed by oversized heads in white coats and sadistic robots. It will be much duller than that. It will be an ocean of ordinariness punctuated by bouts of domestic violence and the occasional trade war. Life will be smoother. The City will grow upwards. Fruit will become large and glossier, the average height and life expectancy of the average *homo sapiens* will improve and boredom, like security and prosperity, will probably increase, to the detriment of literature, which feeds on the plankton of doom. But let us pretend otherwise for a moment, since the railway of progress occasionally hits an obstinate mountain or an impassable river, and the derailing of the trains produces real nightmares, tangible bad dreams, scenarios that seem improbable from the perspective of golden ages but which have a fraudulent attraction, a glamour and secret charm: for there is no question that barbarism and Dark Ages have their mystique and there are signs that the City might take a wrong turn, skid sideways and fall from grace. The peasant has a bad dream that goes with eating too many dates and salted nuts and the dream is called Futuropolis or the Re-invention of the City, a dream that is based, however, on solid empirical facts – because the future, as said, is a cancer and its tumours, lesions and scars are everywhere in evidence.

Well, citizens, you will be glad to know at least that Futuropolis, the land of the rising sun (in several senses, since half of its inhabitants are orientals), has at last perfected the systems that underpin your present way of life and which function with such

97

irritating inadequacy. The drains have been perfected, the plumbing is no longer susceptible to lapses into stenching ataxy, high-speed trains running on magnetic rails overhead have at last stopped the City from looking like a provincial museum and social classes, races and income brackets have been definitely compartamentalized geographically. The entire thirteenth, fourteenth and fifth *arrondissements,* the south-eastern sector of the City, for example, have blossomed into Europe's largest Chinatown, or rather Viet-town, as the descendants of the Boat People erect steel towers of their own radiating out from the heartland of the old Chinatown around the Place d'Italie, monolith commercial centres devoid of any sign of Latin script where the Tang brothers have multiplied their open-air markets and import warehouses and where sampan rice-porridge packs and gleaming tins of oyster sauce rule the shelves under the benevolent aegis of plastic shrines and paper lanterns.

The Avenue d'Ivry itself, where the original Tang supermarket with its Marché Têt used to stand seducing the senses with its alleys stuffed with muskmelon sweets, baithoy candy and arrowroot vermicelli, has long since become a valley of streaked concrete and tinted glass. The Viet Commercial Centre was the first to dare flirt with the future and it is possibly with nostalgia that you will one day look back at the surreal plaza on the top floor, that immense diorama surrounded on all sides by tower blocks and containing at its centre a series of aluminium pavilions in the curving Chinese style under whose pseudo-oriental roofs lurked video shops and family restaurants, all cowering – along with a scum-line of bored teenagers – under the shadow of the towers, oceans of windows receding into the heavens. Who dreamed up this bizarrely cruel form of urban landscaping? With what fine sense of human suffering were these tantalizing pavilions set down under these terrifying skyscrapers? In the restaurants, extended Viet families sit around tables piled with *pâtés imperials* and *saté* soups. Outside, odd faces look harassed and afflicted, scuttling for cover like cockroaches. A bold and chic insectarium! This space was designed to inflict a cockroach complex upon the wretched human bugs who chose to venture there. The first visionary modern designers and architects disclosed the important axiom that the modern man is a cockroach and should be treated as such. And you will be gratified to hear that all needs of cockroach man have been foreseen, that he is attended to by state-sponsored pest controllers, nutritionists, environmentalists, insect lobbyists and of course nuclear engineers: for, as is well known, the noble cockroach is the only animal that can effortlessly survive lethal doses of radioactivity. Your similarity to the cockroach, citizens, is in other words complete and you can thank your urban architecture for this miraculous and timely transformation.

The cockroach, like man, is in favour of order, and so the City has struggled to achieve a crystalline structure on both the small and the large scale. Out of the rotting shambles of the old quarters, sugar cubes of alabaster, cones of metal and pyramids of astonishingly durable transparent material arose, one of them right in the middle of the courtyard of the Louvre. Who did not thank his stars that he had lived to see the end of that atavistic nightmare known as Paris? Who did not feel an impulse to slay oxen in thanks to the gods for having witnessed such transcendent miracles? Order assassinating muck, logic unfolding its wings over ataxy, perspicuity wiping out disorder. Who can have forgotten the epoch-making day in 1965 when General de Gaulle flew in a helicopter over the Greater Paris area in the company of Paul Delouvrier and, after an hour's flight, turned to the latter and declared: 'Delouvrier, remettez-moi un peu d'ordre dans cette bordel!' ('Give me a bit of order in this pigsty!') What brilliant intuition, uttered with such force and precision! Every great head of state should take a helicopter ride over our metropolises! The passion for order has not only resulted in the construction of the new satellite towns such as Cergy-Pontoise and Marne-la-Vallée, built with all the noble utilitarianism of fall-out shelters for the masses, it has invaded the City within the Péripherique as well. Like a wound of optimism, the suburbs of Futuropolis had begun to carve themselves a swathe of territory in the eastern half of the City by the end of the 1970s. Around the Place d'Italie, the cockroach breeding pens were an army on the move: the shopping centre and the Rubis and Beryl towers were the proof of their determination to stay. Only occasionally did the future deign to soften its features, as in the rue des Hautes Formes at the end of the Avenue Edison, where the Moorish blocks joined by overhead arches produced pleasing pale colours at sunset. Into these stalactitic towers reminiscent of Hong Kong the Chinese and Vietnamese moved until even the street signs suddenly disappeared one night and were replaced by new ones handwritten in Chinese script. Murals looking from a distance like *montages* of Maoist socialist realism, though in fact portraying subjects such as plump children riding on the backs of ducks and catfish, appeared on the walls of the old houses in which no one lived any longer. At every intersection glittering video shops materialized out of nowhere and in their windows could be seen all the latest hits of Elvis Phuóng and Kim Ngan arrayed among tinselled marriage gowns and fake Ming vases.

But it was not in the thirteenth *arrondissement* that past and future confronted each other most bitterly in this age. It was in the nineteenth and twentieth that the struggle was at its fiercest and where the outcome for the whole City was largely decided. There is no question who won in the long run, but imagine yourselves in the year 1989 when the issue was still in the balance, when the rue de Belleville still possessed its gracious houses embellished with coats of arms and when the Villa Amélia still boasted its cottages echoing with the songs of birds. But in order to bring home to you what you have lost, we need to digress and imagine a tour on foot of the area around Télégraphe as we would have advised the casual tourist of that age to follow. You will have to use your imagination somewhat, but if you close your eyes and think of old postcards, you should be able to recreate the City in your mind's eye.

Imagine, then, the Place des Fêtes. A circular square with circular gardens at its centre, complete with bandstand and blue elephants, and on certain days of the week a circular outdoor market around the garden. To complete this motif of circles there is in one corner of the square a modern fountain of concentric rings of polished stone interspersed with pebbles donated to the otherwise reviled and despised location by a mayor named Jacques Chirac. Unfortunately the water has been cut off and the high winds on top of this hill blow dunes of rubbish from the market into the pool, which is dry. Our peasant may well have felt nostalgic for the vines and strawberries that used to be grown here or even for the cries of the wild beasts that disturbed the nocturnal calm as late as the 1880s. And what of the dances, balls and celebrations that gave the square its name? Well, it is clear that cockroaches do not dance unless it is underground. In place of the rustic cherry trees are oblong neo-Mussolinian towers in brown and white and the fields of asparagus and barley have disappeared under concrete mini-plazas redolent of certain areas of Warsaw.

Walk along the right hand of the square, however, go through the stark arcade as far as the rue Augustin Thierry, turn left and you will find one of those curious structures that the City's totalitarian development has been unable to uproot: a rotunda of grey stone sunk several feet below ground level and surmounted by a graceful lantern filled with nesting pigeons. You may be aware that François I built his *château d'eau* here and so you will stop out of curiosity. But the structure is hermetic and withdrawn. It has the appearance of a lost barbarian tomb, the resting place of a Visigothic princeling, its outer shell covered with grass and wall plants. Inside, two spiral stairways lead down to a circular cistern fed by three gutters and from one side a large tunnel leads off into subterranean darkness bearing a runnel of fast-moving water. The indecipherable inscription hung above the cistern provides the date 1583, while another, pinned above the tunnel with rusted brackets and written in Gothic script, is all but unreadable. The cistern is filled with the detritus of the City, yellow metro tickets, plastic Evian bottles, twigs, orange peel, Ed grocery bags. The ubiquitous Visigothic graffiti crawls down the walls as far as the tunnel and then hesitates, wondering whether it is worth the risk. Absolute silence reigns with the murmur of water. Another piece of graffiti tooled into the stones records the date 1763. Is this the ancient royal fountain transmogrified into a forgotten crossroads of underground gutters? There is no sign erected at its door, no commemoration or legible plaque. Lost in the landscape of *blockhaus* concrete it slumbers with its secret waters, sinking an inch further into the ground every year. You will leave it behind without a moment's hesitation and make your way to the rue Compans, down which you will turn left and continue as it plunges downward in the direction of the Buttes-Chaumont. But the thought of it will at least give you some unease, a feeling of irresponsible anxiety. You will wonder whether you saw it all, whether it was a hallucination of the worst kind – a genie in the shape of a building.

In any case, you continue down the rue Compans. Half-way down, the new housing of Futuropolis has risen out of the ashes of the slums that once bore witness to the street fighting of the Commune. The giant complex, numbered from the outside simply A1 to A3, is built like a castle, with ivy-covered bastions, portcullis entrance and cavernous hall, a central white block tower equipped with dozens of identical blue blinds and surmounted by the red and white spears of cyclopian aerials. At this time, given the primitive level of urban planning, you can still peer into the slum tenement at no. 55 across the way, a pile of peeling shutters and cramped balconies stuffed with folded ironing boards, plastic potties, strings of infants' socks and bits of piping – and through the open door you can get a glimpse of a trash-filled courtyard with a single tree holding together eight washing lines. The stench of boiled herbs and gusts of Arab music, as well as the dark stares from within, drive you away, no doubt, and so you continue down the rue Compans, gradually becoming aware, however, that Futuropolis has not conquered everything in its path yet and that a curious village atmosphere persists in making itself felt only a stone's throw away from the Place des Fêtes! At the crossroads with the rue de Crimée and the rue Botzaris, at the base of the shark's fin of the Buttes-Chaumont park you turn right up the rue du Général Brunet, increasingly struck with surprise at the peculiar kind of industrial intimacy and suburban quiet that reigns here, and proceed as far as the Place de Rhin et Danube, at the centre of which you will see a smiling representation of a young girl holding a sheaf of corn. The reaction to this apparition can only be amazement. The square itself is as far from Futuropolis as any part of the City without exception, embalmed in the chocolate browns and greys of the small houses, the rows of stunted trees along the avenues around it and the provincial pace of life in its quiet cafés. Exiting from the ovular square by the small rue de la Fraternité, you climb into a high republican village of secluded streets filled with eccentric cottages and suburban houses, all equipped with idealistic and politically quaint names: rue de la Liberté, rue de l'Égalité, Villa du Progrès, and so on. Taking the rue de la Liberté you stumble upon a series of sloping footpaths to your right, pedestrian streets lined with secret houses screened behind walls and hedges of laurels and dog-roses, and here you find the strange Villa Amalia, the Villa de Fontenay and the Villa Marceau. The villas here are never visible and the air, being clear and clean, gives the illusion of the Roman Campagna in spring, an illusion that holds at least as far as the rue de Mouzaia.

Returning more or less by the way you have come, you regain the rue du Crimée and find the quiet rue des Annelets on the far side, which is reached by means of a staircase. And at the end of the rue des Annelets you come across the delicate rue des Solitaires with its miniature Grecian statues in niches and occasional pink house fronted by lonely trees. Turning left here you then find the rue de Palestine and continue to the end towards the rue de Belleville and the neo-Gothic church of St Jean Baptiste, the parish church of Belleville whose twin spires dominated the *quartier*'s skyline until the invention of the principles of Futuropolis.

The triangular space in front of the church formed by the confluence of the rues Belleville, Jourdain, Lassus and Palestine is typical of the city that you have lost: composed, harmonious, adjusted to what the casual eye can absorb without pain. The winding, tumultuous rue de Belleville is as organic as the creeper of a giant tropical plant, self-absorbed and resiliently immune to reason. However, you will not want to follow the rue de Belleville just yet, you will pursue instead the rue de Jourdain as it descends gently towards the small square that joins it to the rue des Pyrénées and then climb the flight of stairs that is the continuation of the rue Levert to the slightly sloping junction of the rue de la Mare, the rue des Cascades and the rue des Envierges. Of all these streets the most unexpected is the rue des Cascades, which bends gradually on its way down to the rue Ménilmontant. Here a distinctly austere and unsophisticated charm is in place. Flights of steps cut into the hillside veer off in imitation of those of Montmartre a century ago, still empty and sunk in pastoral neglect; the ramshackle houses seem submerged in the same rural calm and the little slopes that overshadow the street in places make it even more secluded and stubbornly resistant to change. There is nothing picturesque or gorgeous in these former slum streets, but they are more than symbolic of the City that existed once upon a time, preserving itself through fantastic storms of violence and misery: they are the last streets that are not marching to the lithe, internal rhythms of Futuropolis, they are not moving anywhere, they are standing still within their own laws and they will only be disrupted by force. Returning to the irregular square where the four or five streets converge, you appreciate the imperturbable ethos of neighbourhood, coherence and modesty. Like the rotunda, it must be a fiction, it will burst like a soap bubble and cover your gullibility with ridicule. Down by the Boulevard de Ménilmontant, by the stinking tenements of the rue des Cendriers where women in turbans scour through garbage bins, the cranes and cockroaches in tin hats are busy introducing a healthy note of realism into your romantic nostalgia. For there, within earshot, Futuropolis is growing like a diaspora of mushrooms, the same towers, the same chessboards of minuscule windows, the same drainage works, the same aerials, the same faces behind the glass filled with the same self-pity and boredom, the same empty furrows of recently turned orange earth waiting for eruptions of stone.

Yes, citizens, a strange conjunction of circumstances. Futuropolis had quite a struggle at the beginning, despite its initial triumphs. From time to time barricades were erected in the streets to protest its advance. But the nineteenth *arrondissement*, as in the time of the Commune, had its symbolic side. As soon as the Cemetery of Belleville was walled in, the City knew the time had come to accept the inevitable. And since the guiding principle of the Re-invented City is the subtle and peaceful combination of hierarchy and universal entertainment, who can regret the turning of squalid ghettos into zones of *son et lumière*, the conversion of the St Lazare station, that hangout for cut-throats and footpads, into a high-tech dolphinarium with seventeen species from around the world, or the rehabilitation of the Boulevard de Clichy and the Metro line as far as Barbès into a spooky roller-coaster offering hours of fun and thrill to all the family and at a fraction of the cost of running a train service? The Place des Fêtes is a protected historic area, the Rubis tower is covered in glass to protect it from the atmosphere, the Tour Maine-Montparnasse is in its own museum and the rue des Hautes Formes has been fully excavated and integrated tastefully into an overhead railway station. However, if you are still feeling a little sentimental, and wish – in your all too human way – to pay your respects to your doomed and downtrodden past, why don't we observe, nationwide, a minute's silence in memory of the rue des Cascades, where so many children died of cholera and diphtheria and where the last sadness of the human mind lingered on into the dawn of the new age before finally giving up the ghost in the face of Futuropolis? A minute's silence, then. RIP.

The Small but Magical Universe of Madame Pompom

✠

Our peasant, being an addict of fantasy of any kind, is an avid reader of newspapers and consumes them endlessly while seated at his favourite table at the Café St Jean. What was his surprise, then, when he read the following entry in *Libération*, inconveniently tucked away – as such scandalous stories always are – in the sidelines of the 'Société' page, buried in the middle of the paper between pages twenty and twenty-two?

SHE LEFT HER MOTHER WITH THE DOGS

Pascale Revault, 48, left her four German shepherds with her mother, Madame Odette Pompom, 69, and the latter's live-in boyfriend, Bertrand Salvatti, 72 years. The old lady fell asleep in an armchair and was immediately set upon by the four dogs to the horror of Mr Salvatti, who was too old to intervene. Madame Pompom died under the eyes of her companion. She was partially devoured by the canines. The scene of carnage, in the eighteenth *arrondissement*, was discovered by the *concierge* after the old man had fainted. Experts have concluded that the four dogs were trained to kill but would not normally do so unless threatened or in a state of starvation. The hearing continues.

Why, that's the lady upstairs at no. 37, the collaborator who had her head shaved but who still speaks German to her pigeons! And didn't her daughter, fruit of a liaison with the enemy, die in mysterious circumstances as a child? Who could have passed on such erroneous and abnormal information to the press and at a time when Madame Pompom was never healthier, never more maternally fascistic, never more sad and humane?

It can only be that she did it herself – for Madame Odette Marguerite Pompom, the girl with the plastic roses in her hair at the Chat Noir in the winter of 1943, lives in a private universe that is at once small but magical.

Nevertheless our peasant is concerned about such reported canine barbarities, for of all the inhabitants of no. 37 Madame Pompom is the most similar to what he imagines his alter ego to be should it suddenly assume human form. The reason for this is that the grubby and bombastic old woman is a liar of such fluency and verve that he is unconsciously seized with an almost adulatory admiration for her. And yet she has lied so hard, so concretely, so dramatically, that her lies have come to pass, they have passed from her small but magical universe into the real one.

For example, she is one of those liars who has always been present accidentally at every historically significant drama that has fallen within her lifetime. During the summer of 1938 a famous Hungarian poet was walking down the Champs-Élysées minding his own business when suddenly one of the boulevard trees snapped for no apparent reason and fell directly on to his head, killing him instantly. 'I was right there,' Madame Pompom says, grasping the general area of her heart. 'I saw it fall on to his head – he was wearing a Bomberg hat! I was only eighteen but I knew how to catch their eyes. He winked at me just before he got flattened. In fact, I was the last thing he saw on this earth. Little me!' On another occasion, in 1942, she was standing on one of the platforms of the Barbès-Rochechouart Metro station when the first assassination of a German officer carried out by the French Resistance occurred right under her nose. 'A chunk of brain landed on my knee and a piece of cartilage hit me just above the left eyebrow.' And to this day she will show, not without an element of necrophiliac pride, the 'stain' left behind on her hideous patella by that drop of Gestapo brain tissue.

Like our peasant, she is an avid reader of newspapers, especially the 'Petits Annoncés', which she scours with a still-alert sexuality, drawing rings around 'Young Man seeks Mature Dominator' and 'Little Boy Wants Cruel Mama for Justified Hidings'. In her gloomy little flat where the transistor ceaselessly churns out nauseating accordion music on an obscure wavelength that no one else can find, she sometimes practises a few blows with her whip, for Madame Pompom, that innocent eighteen-year-old eyeing up Hungarian poets on the Champs-Élysées, ended up working in a notorious S&M brothel during the Occupation, flagellating blond conquerors in exchange for silk stockings and five-course meals at the Lido.

Occasionally she wakes up on sunny mornings and refuses, in her subconscious, to acknowledge the passage of forty years, assuming that it is the year 1942 and that the night before she has been thrashing Oberleutnente with thonged whip. She skips around Montmartre in a pair of carpet slippers with the sinister turban on her head and greets the *gendarmes* loitering around the police station at the corner of the rue de la Vieuville with a gay 'Sieg Heil!', seeing them in the fantastic prism of her brain as Wehrmacht regulars. She wanders around the whole city in these carpet slippers. One day the peasant saw her in the chic *chocolatier* Godiva on the rue de la Paix wearing the slippers and the turban and shouting to the girls behind the banks of luxury chocolates: 'It's for Zazou who eats anything but rum centres . . . Herr Kessler will pay next Monday!' and banging her fist into phalanxes of *pralinés*. But by the time she has positioned herself at the bar of the St Jean with her scabby lasa apsa under one arm and a *panaché* in front of her she has recovered from her delicious and delirious daydreams and is content prosaically to plan the dismantling of synagogues, the opening of a luxury whorehouse equipped with suits of armour with inward-looking spikes and hygienic maces for thrusting into anal apertures and the construction of a new dog cemetery which might eventually be extended to accommodate deceased Moslems. Her face, divested of the serene expression that uplifts it when she is back in 1942, is livid, varicose red and puffed up with the doses of Halcion which she pushes up her backside at the wrong time of day and in incorrect quantities. By midnight she is drunk, the lasa apsa has walked home alone in a huff and she is telling groups of German tourists about the splendid physique of that glorious Hun Herr Kapitan Moltke, who took forty blows to the 'lumbago region' without wincing and who could make love for eight hours nonstop while tied upside down to the wall with nailed leather thongs. 'But,' she says, 'they don't make men like that any more, and the German was always, in my opinion, a superior physical being!'

Sometimes, when he is prone to particularly virulent night-mares, our peasant dreams that Madame Pompom has re-ascended to the heights of her former glory, that she has opened a brand-new brothel in Passy modelled on New York's Mineshaft complete with the latest gadgets, though not catering to the specific tastes of homosexuals: gibbets, underwater cages, pillories, racks, thumb-screws, urinals, high-voltage wires. All the girls are dressed in SS uniforms and when timorous clients push the front-door bell of Pompom's Dungeon they are confronted with the apocalyptic vision of the Madame herself swathed from head to foot in wet-look leather, a peaked hat with a skull and crossbones emblazoned above the peak, studded thigh boots and a butch leather jacket barely concealing gigantic, withered breasts. From inside, through a reek of sweat and urine, come male screams and moans and the thud of heavy objects. 'I am Madame Pompom,' she says purringly, 'and this is my little dungeon. Abandon hope, sweety-pies, all who enter here!'

Although he wakes up in panic, his face sweating, he is neverthe-less immediately comforted by the sound of the accordion music booming through the floorboards and the real Pompom's voice shouting to the lasa apsa: 'Not another sardine for the Marshal . . . not yet . . . not until he sits properly on his backsidesy-widesy and sticks out his tongue . . . there . . . does Mummy forget his sardines? No, don't spit it out! Oh, I knew it, you're a traitor! Smacksy-wacksy for bad boys . . . sit! Sit!'

Who can say, either, whether she acts upon her flirtations with the classified ads in the flimsy Paris broadsheets she picks up, like everyone else, in the café? Who can say whether she deliberately disseminates false information among the press or whether she was one of the working and ex-prostitutes invited to appear on the 'Stars à la Barre' television show swathed in black robes and plastic facial masks like a mixture of chador-clad Iranian female sappers and revellers at a Venetian ball? No one charts her mysterious circumnavigations of the City at night, nor the even more sly peregrinations of her shameless imagination. Like a certain kind of once-attractive Parisian woman she is obsessed with tarots, macrobiotics and her own death. He hears her padding above him, repeating softly to herself, or to her dog, or to both: 'They said I'm not going to die . . . the cards say I'm not going to die . . .' And there is a possibility that the cards are correct in not throwing up the Grim Reaper among the combinations she deals out for herself on a small table in her kitchen and that they are right in predicting she will live for ever. The people you suspect of being secretly immortal all have that look in their eye. They know they're not going to die like you.

For a small charge, say a small flattery concerning the condition of her skin or the colour of her eyes, Madame Pompom will draw up for you a peremptory horoscope by means of a large collection of mystic literature, a complete set of eighteenth-century tarots and that indispensable handbook to the secret sciences, Erlich's *The Twelve Initiations of Cosmic Love*. For example, the peasant himself has been given the following definitions written on the back of a cigarette pack:

a) Earth-fixed-Negative.
b) Ruled by Venus and by the planet Pan-Horus.
c) Symbol: the Bull.
d) Night forces: Feminine.
e) If lunar sign is in conjunct, trine or sextant may explore uncharted regions either on earth on in space.
f) Usually limited to Terra Firma, however.
g) May ascend to the finest octave of the Superconsciousness of the Sun Sign if married to a Pluto-dominated Scorpio.
h) Typical 7-7 Sun Sign Pattern.

Madame Pompom is also equipped with a remarkable collection of astrological tapes bought from a mail-order company specializing in the occult resolution of sexual problems. Now as it happens lucky travellers on the Metro sometimes come across small publicity booths in the underground station which advertise these same tapes, with titles like *Premature Ejaculation and Cosmic Cycles*, *Frigid Women and Karma* and *Erections through Hypnosis*. This proves the illimitable demand for the enlightened practitioners of cosmic evolution in this sophisticated technocratic City, a demand which is of course greatest among the educated, high-income, superbly cultured middle class. Have not the erudite works of the Egyptologist-mystic Schwaller de Lubicz (of whom our dear Madame Pompom is an ecstatic fan) sold in their millions? Who has not read *Her-bak pois chiche, Le Roi de la théocratie pharaonique* and *La Lumière du chemin*, all published by the mighty and respectable Flammarion, stupendous verbal edifices of pedantry and gibberish that slide so comfortably down the post-hippy throat? The works of Jean Herbert, Alexandra David-Neel's *Mystiques et magiciens du Tibet*, Shri Aurobindo's *Expériences psychiques dans le yoga* and translations of Gurdjieff adorn the shelves of Madame Pompom, as they do of vast sections of the population. No doubt the latent Hinduism of the swastika seduced her, just as theories of reincarnation and tirades against occidental science thrill her with vistas of eternity and immortality.

Had it not been for her horror of all skins darker than the colour of yogurt, she would have joined forces long before now with the spell-wielding *concierge*, who might have considerably improved her psychic skills. But she lives in her own world, a world breached only by her two spiritualist doctors, the Magicians, who compose her weekly diets by means of a ouija board around which, instead of simple letters, are written vegetarian food stuffs. The glass says carrots for two weeks, biological rice for nine days, broccoli and *nom cuam* until the solstice . . . and the soul, for a small charge, will digest and shit regularly.

But whatever her chances of reaching the age of a thousand intact, our peasant – perturbed and also somehow curiously elated at the thought that she might have been devoured by her daughter's four redoubtable German shepherds – immediately abandons his newspaper at the café table and bounds down the steps of the rue André Antoine to no. 37 to see whether she is still alive, or even – what a thought! – in one piece. He bangs on the door on the first floor. There is a sound of shuffling slippers. So she's alive! The door opens and a foul odour of dogs wafts out on to the landing.

'Yes, they're here,' she says slyly, looking him straight in the eye. 'I'm feeding them sardines. They're so greedy, she doesn't feed them enough. Well, you know what happens when you don't give dogs enough to eat. They get sad.'

Poking his head nosily through the door, the peasant sees, massed in the dim rectangle of her grubby salon decorated with photos of Marshal Pétain and the 21-year-old tank commander from Schleswig-Holstein who made her pregnant in the summer of 1942, the forms of four huge German shepherds engrossed in the act of eating. The curtains are drawn. Madame Pompom is looking radiant, as if she has just stabbed an enemy in the back. And the curious thing is that, from that day on, the little lasa apsa was never seen again.

I Desire Severa

Hardly reseated at his favourite table at the St Jean, with its pile of newspapers, books and periodicals, the peasant, merely turning the page on which he had found the premature tale of Madame Pompom's demise, finds himself hurled into dramas hardly less strange. The Parisian press keeps the bizarre and disturbing stories thrown up by the everyday life of the metropolis half-concealed from the casual eye and it is only by dint of a certain amount of dogged industry that they can be dragged into the open air or even found in the first place. Who would think, for example, that murders are committed almost every day which never reach further than page eighteen of *Libération* and which simply never appear in the otherwise exemplary pages of *Le Monde*? Local and spontaneous eruptions of violence that are fully equipped with all the insolence and bravura of a surrealist silent film.

A man walks into a *boulangerie* and steals a *croissant*: the owner, a young woman, takes out a shotgun and blows out his brains in a fit of pique at seeing her honestly made handiwork disappear down the gullet of a thief. An African with a weak heart taking anti-coagulant drugs is accosted by two mentally handicapped racists who demand his seat and dies from a heart attack on the pavement outside as a result of being pushed to the ground by the two xenophobes, who have just left an asylum. A band of thieves hold up a consignment of stamps. In a street off the Boulevard de Ménilmontant a policeman, having confronted a drugs suspect in a bar, pursues him into an alley, shoots him in the head and then moves the body ten feet before the authorities arrive in order to claim self-defence. The bodyguard of the Jordanian military attaché at Neuilly, a man named Aldahn, is found dead in his own apartment with a 9mm bullet in his head. An employee of Brinks security firm, held by the police in connection with a jewellery robbery at Ivry, is shot dead in the police toilets by an officer who claims 'suicide' until traces of powder from the weapon are found on his fingers. Outside a school in the same Ivry an Arab youth shoots his half-sister and brother because of her affair with a Frenchman. The girl is killed instantly.

Mixed in insouciantly with these garish items the astonished reader stumbles across paragraphs such as the following:

SOS-PIPI

You have a dog but you don't have the time to walk it. Now you can call 'SOS-PIPI', an enterprise started up by four unemployed youths whose professional walkers come to your door and take Fido around the block for a quarter of an hour. For 240 francs you get a monthly subscription comprising 24 walks. To assure those dog-owners who fear theft of their animals, all walkers of 'SOS-PIPI' carry an identity card bearing their photograph. Another precaution: the day before the first walk a meeting is arranged between walker and dog in order to avoid all possible incompatibilities, whether of character or of smell . . .

Or else:

CAN CHOCOLATE BE PORNOGRAPHIC?

The debate is already under way concerning an Italian entrepreneur who has just unveiled bars of chocolate representing the 32 basic positions of the Kama Sutra at a sweet fair. The director of the hotel where the bars were exhibited has declared that he would never have rented his vestibule if he had known such filth was going to be shown there. The entrepreneur, Georgio Balladini, director of Kama Sutra Fine Chocolates has said that only 'philistines' could interpret these erotic scenes as pornographic.

In truth, our lazy rustic is no longer much interested in the international or national news, the results of elections – to which twenty-page pull-outs are devoted – or the inside stories of multi-national takeovers and mergers . . . unless it be some terrorist outrage committed in the olive belt or reports of monk-beatings in Tibet and the execution of television announcers in revolutionary Iran. No, it is precisely the columns of gruesome trivia that fascinate him and which have him glued to his chair for hours on end. And if it is not the titbits of gossip which explore the outer reaches of human depravity, it is the classified ads at the back of the paper, or better still, in the weekly small ads paper, *Paris Boum*, and its various rivals, which are available in all cafés free of charge.

The entries themselves are charged with a laconic lyricism which, needless to say, is entirely lacking in the sports page or the shares index. The language is cryptic and full of furtive ellipses, shot through with exotic anglicisms and imbued with a kind of pornographic nakedness that reminds our reader for some reason of the buffet of a self-service restaurant.

MAN 40 years, would like to make the fantasies of his girlfriend (36, lovely brunette) come true with the help of 2–3 males, 40–50 years, virile and well endowed, no scruples, discreet. Necessary meeting arrange scenario without her knowing taking her through progressive stages of desire to orgiastic fuck without violence and my participation. Sodomy excluded.

ARE WORDS ENOUGH TO LOVE YOU? I prefer the leather against your skin, the kind that burns, the anxiety in your eyes that defy and subjugate me, the necklace around your neck, the one you wear in the lights of the city, and the other one which makes you more dog-like in the secrecy of our nights . . . I'm 40 years old. Dare to raise your pen.

PARIS: CRUNCHY BLONDE, CRISPER THAN A CRACKER, lighter than a chip, less fat than a crêpe, affectionate but not clinging, needs gourmet to devour her under the sun of spring. Tenderness, humour and sensuality will preside at the bacchanalia of spring. The gourmet will naturally have a telephone. Long live spring, love and music! Signed: Flodorissima.

SPANKING. Does receiving or giving a spanking bother you? 43 years, single, nice eyes, agreeable physique, refined, equilibrious,

I've acquired experience in submission without violence. Women having shared in this complicity confess to having experienced bliss. I'm looking for you, Madame, Mademoiselle, I want to listen to your desires for submission or domination, share spanking together. Respect, discretion.

MUSKETEERS? D'Artagnan seeks an Aramis, transvestite, ugly, virile, would like to cross his sword with younger man, svelte, cosmo, BCBG, muscled, moustaches, in nocturnal duels. Antipth. mil. homo. Individualists. Exhibit. maso. welcome. Dream of golden hair in curls, *nuits de la pleine lune*. Leave behind your fears.

But even more than these elliptical odes of forbidden and excruciating pleasures, it is the boxes advertising telephone sex and Minitel dating agencies that arouse the greatest *frisson* in the heart of our peasant voyeur, and in particular that which contains the surly and sultry, the languid and admonishing face of that particular telephone goddess who goes by the name of 'Severa'.

It is only, however, in the Metro that you ever see Severa in all her glory, for it is only there that the publicity posters are in colour. Only there can you see the unnerving redcurrant colour of her hormonally inflated lips – lips which are thick, contemptuous and unsmiling – the dull gold of her hair and the slight vanilla tint of her skin. And the face, instead of the measly and unsatisfactory little monochrome image that you get in the newspaper, is gratifyingly enlarged to terrifying proportions. She is designed to give you delicious nightmares from which you will never escape while your testicles are active, her blown-up grey eyes are like the eyes of a giant cruel cat looking through your wretched little mousehole and waiting to eat you alive.

SEVERA

36.15

Le Dressage Commence

Yes, she is longing and willing to whip your little behind and stick a bull whip down your throat! She will happily and gracefully grind your face into the dust with a screwing motion of her fang-like heels. You pick up the telephone – for the danger of Severa is that she is only a voice, the voice of the image you know and love so well – and nervously dial the Minitel code that puts you in direct contact with her. You are certainly not alone in your obsession: our peasant says to himself over and over in the bathetic depths of his unconscious, 'I desire Severa!', a phrase he obviously shares with millions of others.

You wait nervously while the telephone rings. Four rings and then there is a click as the receiver is lifted off the hook and the mute pause of a recorded message. But the message, to your unease and surprise, is not recorded. The voice of Severa herself comes on to the line.

'Je vous écoute, ne soyez pas timide, vous êtes coquin, je le sais . . .'

A dark, granular voice . . . what else?'

You mutter obscenities.

'Ah ouais t'es cochon, toi!'

So suddenly you are a 'tu'. You grew bolder. You tell her what you think about her lips and that vanilla colour of hers.

'T'es plus chien que moi alors, j'adore tes cochonneries, répete-les, ne sois pas gené, chéri, ça c'est pas la peine, tu le sais . . .'

In your sly, slippery, proletarian French you caress the back of her neck. You say surprising things. You get your money's worth. You get worked up. You look deep into your bilingual dictionary.

'Mais t'es décidement pas pédé, toi, ranconte-moi tout, faut pas cacher tes secrets, Severa est très curieuse, elle imagine tout, elle veut savoir . . . t'as été méchant, ça elle le sais bien, t'as fait des choses bien dégueulasses . . .'

In your halting argot you dare to ask her for a rendezvous – what do you think you're doing, as if a pro like Severa . . . ! But before you have time to stop yourself, apologize or in any other way cover your tracks, she increases your amazement by accepting.

'T'as du génie au téléphone!' she explains coyly.

She suggests that you meet her at the Porte de Vanves Metro station: a strange place to meet, you think, near the end of the line! What if it's a joke? But Severa seems genuine. She cajoles and flirts. She finishes work on the phone at midnight. She'll be in a white BMW 320 (what else for Severa?) You put down the phone in a sweat of panic. Is it true? Has the telephone lied as it usually does? The vanilla throat, the white convertible, the mission to please, the fetid vivarium of fantasy . . . there is only one thing to do. You put on your shoes, cover your neck with *eau de toilette* and rush out into the night to catch the next Metro train. But before you reach your heart's desire you will have to descend into that realm which, as much as any part of the City, is as great a magnetic field of the imagination as Severa herself, and which might easily divert you before you reach your dubious destination: the Metro. You enter this cave world unarmed, with a certain amount of trepidation. 'I desire Severa!' you mumble, clattering through the computerized stiles and heading earthward into humid tunnels and intersections. You have apparently forgotten that, like the Metro, your one-night goddess is used by everyone as readily as a toothbrush. There are no exceptions in the City of fantasy: everyone is exactly the same, and after only a minute in the Metro you suddenly realize the fact. The Metro, like dreams and sex, is the great leveller.

Lost Souls

After his calamitous experience with the world of small ads, the peasant – in order finally to escape from birds and bees, the cruel and squawking cannibalism of sex – decides to make a move in the direction of some artistic landscape . . . why not the Andy Warhol festival that's showing at the République, or an art gallery filled with four-inch tapestries woven from crude ethnic tufts of Peruvian llama hair in basketweave frames? There is something lonely and nomadic in those chic watering holes which cannot be found on maps, which resemble nothing if not the shifting campsites of desert tribes. He is in need of the contemporary, in its pithy, grained, lugubriously unsentimental form. He wants a sly and civilized kick in the throat.

Full of hope, therefore, he charges down to the Action République, the gloomiest *avante-garde* cinema, where there is always a scruffy and forlorn line of semiotics professors and black-leather intellectuals with the crazed look of suicidal jerboas in their eyes, and rushes in to catch the latest in the Warhol run, *Lonesome Cowboys*, which – if we are reluctantly to come clean – he rudely mistook for a raunchy homo porn feature, along with *My Hustler* and *Nude Restaurant*. Not only that, but once tightly wedged into the fourteenth row between two burly and sudorific *aficionados* who will not tolerate even the slightest sound that will detract from their enrapturement, he is condemned to sit through all three films in one sitting, a torment which is not even alleviated by the punctual and frivolous appearance between two features of buxom, foaming ice-cream girls dressed in black stockings and flounced *décolletés*.

'Wouldn't you like to run barefoot through his golden locks?' the fag voyeur of *My Hustler*, observing a blond beach boy from afar, asks his whining female friend.

'Do the flies bother you?' someone drones.

'Oh, you bitch.'

'You filthy fag.'

'His golden hairs!'

'The beach . . .'

'The penknife . . .'

'Adonis.' Exasperated sighs, quiet voices.

'Your end is open, I know sweetheart, and your other end . . .' suppressed sniggers.

'From one fag to another . . .' Noises off, waves, cocktail glasses.

And so on.

With the satisfied grunts and chortles of the *cognoscenti* sitting unpleasantly in his ears, the peasant finally breaks loose and shoots upstairs to relieve himself, then carries on into the street without waiting to see the conclusion of *My Hustler* or the further cavortings of Taylor Mead and Brigid Berlin or whatever other denizens of the Factory are now being hurled into the eyeballs of the jerboas, and as soon as his lungs are immersed in fresh air, he regrets his decision and the absence of masochism that now lies ahead of him. He goes home hoping for a miracle. And as it happens it is his lucky day, for just as he opens his door, his brain still marred by the Warhol lucubrations, he sees a small and effete pink envelope lying, or rather reclining, on his doormat, an envelope so dainty and busy with clever little graphics that he knows immediately it is from a stranger.

Now, whereas the three films of Warhol have come from a world which elicits a natural curiosity among Parisian audiences but which in their tone and style are glacially alien to it, the pink letter is definitely from *within*. As he upturns it a thick card pops out spiced with an Annick Goutal perfume called L'Heure Exquise. To his amazement, it is an invitation. A *vernissage*, an opening of sculptures in a loft by the Canal de l'Ourcq, for that very night.

BENOIT IZO

sculptures de chewing

is all it says, and the address underneath. The card is bright pink and fragrant, like a baby's tongue. *Sculptures de chewing.* Izo. Why, he has completely forgotten – the slant-eyed boy he ran into in the queue for *Masturbation no. 2*, or was it *The Chelsea Girls*, the one who smelt like a girl and never stopped masticating gum! So, he's a sculptor! It only shows that regular attendance at the Warhol festival at the Action provides indispensable introductions in the slippery and often stagnant realm of social intercourse. He puts on his round embroidered black cap, his black camel pants and leather jacket and takes the Metro to Jaurès, from where it is a pleasant and eerie walk along the redeveloped canal to the block of lofts that rises abruptly from the water along the Quai de la Loire not far from the point where the rue de Crimée crosses it.

Benoit Izo's loft is as large as a football field, with chocolate-coloured bricks and panels of rough plaster hanging pregnantly in space. There is a small fish tank in the corner, lit by a halogen spot and containing a single bearded carp which circles what looks like a small volcano made of dog biscuits. Over the murmur of a large crowd whose knees are flexing to its rhythm, the rap of Scott La Rock is turned up loud to impair the exchange of opinion.

The peasant – extremely shy and nervous among crowds of strangers – nevertheless has his way of detaching objects of interest from chaotic backgrounds: a Brazilian in a red dress he has seen before, dancing with her African husband with flips of the hip that try politely to suggest the ghetto, the pale Little Boys in knickerbockers and Pee-Wee Herman schoolboy caps and painted carmine lips who sit with crossed legs and pine for other Little Boys who are unfortunately accompanied by grown-up women, the knots of Japanese youth (Izo's bed-fellows?) always in black, those languorous exiles from the land of worker-hoplites who seem to be perpetually amazed by the continued existence of things such as charm and idleness and who drift through what they apprehend as the last U-Kiyoye, Floating World, on earth . . . a dreamworld of non-utility which one day is going to explode in their faces and hurl them back into the real world of Sanyo tape-recorder production lines and Dai-ichi Kangyo-style mega-banks. And there is the host himself, yes, the same bubble-gum fetishist from a few nights before, the same delicate Eurasian face and blackish lips, the same lop-sided haircut and black slip-on plimsoles. He is talking rapidly and energetically. He is opening his mouth and showing his audience something inside, his tonsils maybe or his latest fillings, and tipping his head so that they can see, talking, explaining, chattering. And above the thunder of Scott La Rock, it is even possible, if you strain with all your might, to catch the odd word or phrase of the remarkable and brilliant artist Izo as he delivers unrepeatable insights into . . . *les sculptures de chewing*.

'The mouth is taboo . . orality is taboo, by chewing I communicate with the unconscious. Gum is my elastic mode of intimacy with the Unknown. Gum is not just gum. It is Matter. It is Mystery. It is God. It is Life itself. It is anything you want. The only food that is chewed exclusively for its own sake, it reveals the ultimate and satisfying enigmas of mastication!'

They are listening intently and nodding their heads. They are thinking for the first time in a long while about their mouths, a part of the anatomy they had forgotten all about as far as theory goes. And now along comes the pretty and iconoclastic Izo and revises all their inherited notions about mouths. It's thrilling and sinister at the same time. Now he is telling them about the material for his sculptures, how he was brought to consider the contents of his mouth as a fit subject for art and what it means to be put in immediate tactile intimacy with the mouth of the Other. He explains to them – with many brilliant Eurasian smiles in between – how he chews a piece of gum for weeks without spitting it out, keeping it there even while he sleeps, swims, defecates, refusing to remove it even during love making. In this way, the banal bolus of mass-produced gum acquires something of himself that is unique – and he's not just referring to his enzymes. The gum becomes literally one of his 'organs'. It is Izo in miniature. After three weeks it is removed in this precious condition like a rare port and placed upon a square of black galvanized steel not unlike the bottom of a Teflon frying pan. The process of sculpture is ready to begin.

Izo's chewing-gum pieces have been extensively featured in women's magazines and the world's art quarterlies, where they have been bathed in soft and venereal lights, shot from exquisitely unconformist angles and placed provocatively in marble bathrooms and Scandinavian kitchens.

'The subversion of eating, of the functional, heterosexual, sanitized mouth. A rejection of the conformity of the bourgeois mouth and its equally immoral food. I am putting the whole oral–social order in question. Just a piece of gum . . . but . . . look closely . . . consider . . . examine . . .'

Yes, he's right. He has a point there. We're all guilty with our mouths. So if only we could rip them out and install other mouths instead, pure, minimal and ahistorical mouths, mouths untainted by any form of gastronomy-based imperialism! But since this is impossible, we can at least search our souls by means of Izo's suggestive 'Zero Gum' series, or the mutilated and tormented post-nuclear imagery of 'Spearmint Apocalypse nos. 4–18'.

But the peasant is drifting, feeling his mouth drifting uncomfortably away from his head, and, drawn by curiosity to the walls of the loft where he has unconsciously noticed vague black squares hanging against the white, he detaches himself from Izo and gravitates towards the work. For the black squares are sculptures pinned to the wall, vertically protruberant forms which militate against the facile assumptions of the party-goer. There are dozens, if not hundreds of them. They bear the shape of the artist's mouth, dentures and soul. Innocently, and becoming more and more absent-minded, he follows them round the walls until he comes to the light switch near the elevator door and there, stuck with what looks like deliberate irony, is a scrappy piece of chewing gum plastered by a single thumb on to the steel plate that holds the illuminated recall button. The print of the thumb is clearly visible. The peasant hesitates. Should he or shouldn't he? Faced with this piece of buccal excrement, he is overwhelmed by the habits of a lifetime and by residual instincts of civic propriety. He wants to scrape it off. His hand itches. But in reality he is not thinking twice about it: he reaches out immediately and peels it with some difficulty away from the metal, rolls it with disgust at the thought of someone else's saliva and flicks it on to the floor, where it lies shamefully like a disgraced and ancient bird dropping.

But hardly has he done this when he notices, out of the corner of his eye, a black shape hurtling towards him through the throng of acolytes and party-goers, a black arrow that is aimed directly at him and travelling almost at the speed of light. And before he has turned completely he sees that, yes, it is Izo himself rushing in his direction with an uplifted, admonishing, blenched index finger, his hair sticking out all over with fury and a hysterical reprimand in his eyes, and that the crowd is parting before him as he races from one end of the loft to the other, spluttering uncontrollably: 'What are you doing? What are you doing? My "Caucasian Tonsil"! What have you done with it? I can't believe it . . . I can't believe you . . .'

And he stops like a grief-stricken mother in front of the little turd of gum on the floor. He blubbers.

'I feel raped,' he announces.

The barbarian who has committed this act of sacrilege, tantamount to the sacking of the library of Alexandria, decides to make a clean getaway and summons the lift. In the general chaos of hurt and indignation no one notices him blushing as he disappears into the industrial elevator and hurriedly closes the door, and he is able to descend without too much furore, although it is safe to assume that the talented and charismatic host will not be inviting him back for the opening of his 'gum situations' at the Palais de Tokyo in three years' time.

On the ground floor he finds himself alone. The music has receded to a whisper. It is half-dark outside, a crepuscular dimness that is made superficial by a half moon. As he strides with relief out of the building, however, he is stopped suddenly in his tracks by a deep and grainy voice hailing him from somewhere in the dark . . . a low brick wall to the side of the building, where stacks of concrete mix in plastic bags sit untidily with padlocked hulks of machinery and a row of scaffolding poles leaning over a tar boiler. There is someone by the wall dressed in something with brilliant yellow spots.

'Eh, Dead Man,' the voice calls and hisses – but it is the hiss of a can of spray paint. The figure emerges . . . a fantastical African in a leopard-skin coat who only a moment before was in the thick of Izo's party. He is holding a canister dripping with red paint and on the wall behind him is a lurid word sprayed in chunky capitals with carefully articulated shadows.

The African booms: 'I am Africa Soleil. Long live Africa!'

And suddenly the peasant remembers – the miles of graffiti that cover the city now: he has seen those letters before. The African is drunk on Izo's punch but the moon has brought out his lucid spirit of rebellion and, not caring to waste any more of his time, he has decided to descend into the streets, as he does every night – though not, of course, in his party gear – and paint them.

'It's war, Dead Man,' Africa Soleil announces, titubating and holding up the spray can as if he is about to squirt his revolutionary red aerosol paint into the peasant's eyes. 'Afrika Bambataa has said: the Sun is Power, Africa is the home of civilization as many white children of knowledge have attested in their words, Aristotle is black and Egypt is his mother, peace and harmony spring forth from Africa's sacred womb, the oldest human bones are of Africa as it is said in the scrolls, the locusts of domination will know the wrath of the sun, Paris will be drowned in red sand, the earth will swallow her up, she will disappear at one with Babylon and the children of the Africa-sun will cover with their laughter, it is near the end, as all history teaches the children, the end will begin with the rebirth of the home of homes, the old mother of the human species, progenitor of all languages, Africa the great, Africa the eternal, Africa Soleil!'

His eyes are yellow and devoid of irony and as he booms, sending waves of resonant rhetoric up into the air, the peasant begins to float with him into the astounding fantasy world of that world-prophet Afrika Bambataa, whose empire has established itself in the heart of Paris in the form of a gigantic ocean of words, the ocean of graffiti.

From whichever angle it is considered, there is no question that the City is Europe's greatest open-air monument to graphomania.

It is the Shrine of Bambataa . . .

It is the Capital of Graffiti.

Afrika Bambataa

It will be difficult for the archaeologists of the future to reconstruct the City of the late twentieth century without the aid of scholarly lexicons devoted to the arcane symbols of the underground art of tagging, or graffiti painting, and without a deep and sympathetic understanding of this rich and delicate tradition, their knowledge of the metropolis of the late-industrial Dark Ages will remain perfectly inadequate. What will be their surprise, moreover, when they first discover these underground caves covered as far as the eye can see with the exquisite frescoes of Bambataa, as they will be known to future art historians, with their febrile strength of line, their heady eroticism and voluptuous range of primary colours? Any assumption that this City was no more than a semi-barbarous agglomeration of illiterate, over-rated tribal clans eking a living from desultory trade in slaves and gold will be demolished at a single stroke. They will be stirred to tears by the greatness of these works in the difficult medium of spray, moved to boundless admiration by their ethnic integrity and swept away by their inner logic and architectural vigour. The allegation that this was a primitive and backward culture will instantly be rendered laughable. And from then on the sacred words of these lucid and courageous masters of spray engaged in the decipherment of the mysteries of the non-rational will have to take their place in the vocabulary of all spiritual, sympathetic, sensitive and culturally pluralistic educated people: Afrika Bambataa, Yo Homeboys!

But now the City itself is not so certain of itself. On all its external and internal surfaces, in the Metro, in the suburbs, on the museums, on buses, along the fences of construction sites, a new art is born from the ashes of an obsolete social order. The disinherited of the City rise up, not with rifles and grenades, but with canisters of spray paint, and take their revenge against the

137

Age of Progress, which so cruelly ignores them. Responding to this cry from the heart of the marginalized masses, swarms of warm-hearted journalists, academics and cultural prophets descend with rapture into the streets and discover the true visual pulse of their age. In this immense imagistic diarrhoea surging up from the depths of who knows where they find the 'social transversality', the elusive and entirely successful anarchism and street credibility of which they have been dreaming through long sleepless nights since their own half-forgotten youth. With painful diligence, they learn the cryptic language of the taggers, the nocturnal 'defacers' of the Metro whose superb strokes and designs they feel as the cutting edge of their own emasculated indignation. Tagging has muscle and guts: the fact that some taggers take time off to commit *VAVs* (rapes with violence) lends ideologically unsound but undeniably authentic tones to their graphitic effusions. B. Boys, Fly Girls, Zulus, Troops, Sticks, the Juice, Tags, the *Mouvement* . . . the society of taggers, those who paint tags (codenames), are organized along the hidden lines of fanatically precise definitions. The Zulu Nation, the umbrella society encompassing them all and imported into France by Afrika Bambataa, has its own kings and queens, and although tagging is prohibited by them, the stick (an adhesive strip which can be removed) is permitted. But what is the relation between the *Mouvement* and the Zulu hip-hop tribe? A question of considerable theological nuance, especially since to be or not to be a true Zulu is a question of social life and death for the peripatetic tagger artist. Our armies of palpitating experts have not yet resolved this delicate and complex problem, nor the relation of Zulu hip-hops to definite visual styles. The carefully cultivated individualism of these artists of the night confounds simplistic and facile generalizations.

The unique and irreplaceable opacity of each tag, a personalized emblem only loosely inscribed within the wider order of the *Mouvement*, cannot but be respected in the most scrupulous, the most lavish way! For example, the 'E's of SD Four, with their feline elegance and exemplary wit, have nothing in common with those of Massad, though both belong to the DCMs, Da Criminel Minded. And the elastic ferocity of the DCM Style in turn has little to do with the sophisticated 'troops' (inflated letters) of the TDS (The Destroyers of Subway) or the demagogic *élan* of the

Karai, all of whom, however, orbit around the centre of gravity of the *Mouvement*. As for the highly prized 'F's of Esprits Morts or the 'H's of 93 MC, as is well known, they are now collectors' items on a footing with the fossilized 'sticks' of the TCG (The Crime Gang). How can we underestimate the daring creativity, the explosive and ironic language of anger that this age produced almost in spite of itself? As in the Renaissance, influences cross the seas and inseminate distant lands – so that far away in New York the black DJ Afrika Bambataa, the Michelangelo of the Subway, Lenny McGurr, and the revolutionary sledgehammer pulse of Public Enemy have winged their way across the ocean and come to roost in the searching minds and hearts of the young Zulus and Homeboys of the twentieth *arrondissement*.

It is surprising in this context to note that, given the hysteria greeting the news that the Institut Pasteur will henceforth be publishing its journal in English, and given the general growing bolshiness of the apostles of francophonia (particularly those in the New World), no one in the Académie Française or the press has expressed the least indignation or alarm concerning the massive linguistic, visual and musical invasion emanating from the United States under the aegis of rap and tagging. Entire sections of French youth have defected. Skewed baseball caps, razor-patterned hair, Reebok trainers, flak jackets: perfect reproductions, with all the felicitous and exact rendering of detail you would expect in a Musée Grévin waxwork, of black suburban American youth, Homeboys hot out of the crib. On the airwaves, Radio Nova spews out the sounds of the Bronx, imported DJs, no doubt friends of the immortal Afrika, enable the B. Boys of Paris to perfect their phraseology and accent, and the grammar of Futura thrives, ten years on, in the City that always has one eye on its transatlantic cousin. The new generation of twelve year olds, taking upon themselves the mantle conferred by their illustrious elders, inherits without inner obstacle the ethos of charming hedonism pioneered by their models. As our phalanxes of gushing journalists assure us, *le tag* is a vehicle for the consummation of a certain desire for danger and self-assertion. Its highest aim is pleasure and dominance. The tag is a mark of a personal, dominating identity. Your tag is your soul. Beyond the loose order of the *Mouvement* or the Zulu Nation the tagger exists in an intense world of honour and shame formed by a multitude of bustling, self-important, lethal egos – the crushed and therefore hyper-sensitive ego of the ghetto. The establishment of an international uniform – High-Topped Reebok trainers or Nike Air Jordans, coloured laces undone, Bermuda jean shorts and Spanish hairnets – has not yet obviated this fact. On the contrary. Every tagger knows he is an imperturbable will, an unrecognized genius and the wearer of a sexual organ bigger than anyone else's. The City has incubated its deformed egos and it is only natural that, breaking out of the latrine of anonymity where they have been forcibly kept, they take revenge not only on people but on buildings as well. In naked walls they see the signature of a hierarchy that laughs at them. The laughter is loud and clear. The response is swift and immediate: the rising tide of nonsense, of brain-dead writing.

The Nation-Dauphine line is notorious, although only four stations are actually submerged in graffiti. Barbès, La Chapelle, Jaurès and Stalingrad, the stations along the line that skirts the Goutte d'Or and reaches into Belleville. Even the girders of the overhead bridges connecting the stations are covered with black and red scrawls crammed into every available space. The stations themselves have been turned into temples of tag. The RATP's counter-attack, armed with its anti-graffiti varnishes, has not yet reached into this heartland area of scriptural revolt and the passengers here stand silently in awe of the explosion of graphomaniacal barbarism. Idly they probably wonder how the little buggers manage to get into tunnels (swinging like apes along the wires?) or up to the high vaults which are seemingly inaccessible to anyone not equipped with a five-ton crane. Their blank faces, however, register nothing. The language of tag is entirely feudal and hermetic. A tagger sees one line in the wrong place, put there by a rival, and he is ready to kill. But the non-tagger is only aware of a vague aggression, the squirming face of youth spitting over him and displaying – in a gesture of profound exhibitionism – the nauseous toilet of his brain. If the City is dying in the eyes of the countless factional moralists who ride its public transport system, the reams of writing on the wall are the lesions and pustules on the corpse. No doubt it is for this reason that from time to time large green posters appear overnight on the city walls with the rubric:

AFRIKA BAMBATAA

INCH' ALLAH!

Within twenty years, it is certain, France will be an Islamic
republic.

Hussein Mossawi
Chef Hezbollah d'Amal islamique

The latter, somewhat suspect, title does not detract from the
note of alarm sounded by this purportedly bona fide declaration,
especially as it often appears in the middle of a sea of graffiti.
The City, which sits so solidly and humanely in the realm of the
visual, refusing to violate any of the delicate laws of perspective,
has seen its surface break up gradually – here and there – into
suppurations and weals, blisters, pock marks and multitudes of
sores. The physical props of the metropolis – naturally routinely
despised by the Druids of the Future and the spitting prophets
of the deluge to come – become the theatre of a dissolution into
tribal activism. What giant strides forward! What a bloodying
of the nose for world reaction! You can only imagine (with a
few quietly superior titters on the side) the volcanic feelings of
impotent rage, racial–class anguish and profound national *malaise*
that this bold and hardy development must inevitably arouse in
the hearts of the ridiculous, foul and erstwhile complacent *petit
bourgeoisie* of this Babylon of the Western world! How your heart
leaps for joy at the mere thought of it! What a hard-nosed victory
in the face of impossible odds! Look at them so visually humbled,
so deflated by the simple fact of aesthetic aggression . . . what a
masterful strategy to have discovered: cultural guerrilla warfare by
means of the eyes! We seriously doubt whether any ideologue, no
matter how committed or inventive, could have done better than
that. The City is going the way of all flesh while a new world
is literally coming into being in front of our eyes. Imagine the
brave new world: Yo Homeboys! A sea of multi-coloured letters
. . . pounding rhythms . . . warring, aerosol-wielding tribes of
cultural mutants . . . and no nuclear war first, either!

The collective mental vaginas of the liberal intelligentsia (following the lead of their American colleagues, who have an admirable genius for radical lechery) become glutinous and aroused
not because the art of Bambataa is going to exterminate them
(though this also is undeniable), but rather because the world

which created and supports them – which they naturally loathe with a deep and visceral fury – is going to disappear. The very idea is so exciting on a genital-primitive level that they begin furiously masturbating themselves to help the process along, the achievement of a vast politico-social orgasm in which all their petty hatred, fears, inferiority complexes, revenge impulses and self-detestation will be finally and serenely dissolved. Whipped into gratifying bouts of cultural self-immolation, their cerebral equipment begins to lubricate itself and give off salty juices of despair. Smacking their lips, they produce long and lugubrious catalogues of apocalyptic signs, auguries of doom that can be supported by warehouses of statistics. But the figures do not matter . . . what matters is the gut feeling, the evidence of the senses. The eye has been conquered. 'Look around you' is the advice that subdues. The rising evidence of decay, the graffiti on the walls, everywhere around us. The palpitations of pleasure that result from observation of imminent extinction! The warriors of Bambataa are eventually going to shove Kalashnikovs up our backsides and pull the trigger. It's all we deserve – the sooner these handsome Man Fridays in Spanish hairnets do it, the better! It's all we deserve, it's everything our collective guilt leads to . . . there's no escaping our destiny, the destiny of pink and vulnerable backsides waiting to be raped from behind, spiritually sodomized by the punks in skewed baseball caps, the Zulus of the future! As long as it happens sooner rather than later and in the quiet of a mental boudoir hung with satin sheets. We all believe, with the primitive faith of all lapsed biblical sermonizers, in the power of writing on the wall.

The graffiti-hungry intellectual can, in Paris, satisfy his thirst for signs of the Apocalypse for which he is so ardently waiting simply by strolling through any neighbourhood he chooses. But, as in the Metro, in some places the grapholalia is greater than in others. The suburbs in particular are the scene of chaotic risings, popular rebellions of the word. The entrails of construction sites and the endless miles of industrial wall space offer the insolent armies of urchin taggers ample room in which to exorcize their demons. Insurrection is widespread and unstoppable. The intellectual is hurled into paroxysms. 'Look around you!' If he dares to imagine the future he can hardly fail to include these kilometres of grotesque figures in the generally abominable urban landscape. His social voyeurism is titillated, as is the sense of décor of equally large armies of fashion photographers, who descend every week into the hell-holes of tagging to find the perfect post-Crash background to the latest Kenzo pants. And in the heart of the City itself this fantastic landscape has already made its début, and not only along the Boulevard de la Chapelle from where, riding in the comfort of the overhead Metro, you can see vast holes in the stonework of the City covered with lurid signs and creatures of the imagination . . . in more secret places, too: otherwise unnoticed boils in the City's skin where a continual visual serum flows day and night, beetling accumulations of bastard words and exhortations, Masonic jibes and counter-jibes, explosions of sub-literate rage and infantile jubilation. The writing makes them dead zones, as if finalizing a process which it has ended up by controlling. For example, in that lost corner of the Marais between the rue Beaubourg, the rue de Turbigo and the rue Chapon, dominated by the cafés and Chinacos of the City's least-known Chinatown, the empire of graffiti has created a province which, untypically, is itself threatened by the advent of the Orientals and a certain amount of reactionary bourgeoisification.

At no. 24 rue des Gravilliers a passage opens through a virtually disused doorway and leads to a long L-shaped courtyard at the centre of a towering block of condemned tenements. The 'street' finally makes an exit on the rue des Vertus, but not before it has traversed scenes worthy of the backstreets of Beirut. A notice stuck to the Vertus doorway announces the imminent destruction of the entire block (July 1989) and the cutting-off of water and electricity three weeks before. Along the rue au Maire the northern side of this huge squatters' rat hole presents an impressive and curiously Gothic black stone wall of alarming dimensions. Inside, enclosed and protected from the outside world, desultory gangs hang around in the courtyard or run like thousands of rodents through the rotting passages, stairwells and corridors that riddle this nightmarish edifice. Burnt-out cars litter the cobbled alley that leads from the rue des Gravilliers, while by the former *concierge*'s office can be read the now useless words 'Cour de Rome' and the faded sign of Wang Sang the carpenter. And everywhere, on every available surface, squeezed even on to the oxidized ribs of the burnt cars, the graffiti have arrived like a swarm of locusts. The huge peeling walls of the tenements are covered from top to bottom. The stinking stairwells are covered with a thick carpet of entwined letters. The immense block of stairs receding upwards like a Piranesi incubus by the Vertus doorway is a vertical totem of scrawled tags. Hundreds of eyes peer through the smashed windows on all sides: the cockroaches of the City of the Dead. In this way the leper colonies of the past, and those of the future, were and will be designed. As a stranger enters there is a ripple of eyes, a murmuring far away and the scattering of insect legs. The stranger is prey and he is watched accordingly. If the swarms descend the stairs he will have to run for the street, so he moves carefully and quietly. On all sides he is surrounded by a vertiginous mass of graffiti, of a density and an unrelenting depth that is terrifying. There is no escape from it. If the art of defacement ever needed a city to show to an astonished world its radical, alternative vision of the future, this would be it. The edifice of garbled pseudo-writing crowds in upon the casual stroller, reducing him quickly to a state of paralytic incontinence. Probably there are corpses in the cars and their faces, too, are covered with cryptic tags. You can imagine the artists admiring their own work as they look at the painted faces:

'C'est mortel!'

'Ouai . . . un vrai trip . . .'

'Mieux qu'un cutter!'

'Toyer c'est enculer . . .'

'Mortel, le truc.'

And so on: the staccato language of babes . . . the language of bright young roaches good with their hands. A new art is born with an original vocabulary, and who are we to sneer at it when all the historical evidence accumulated by our legions of industrious experts demonstrates without a shadow of a doubt that tagging, the weird and tardy fruit of subway art, is the dominant aesthetic form of this peculiar century? Although the bulldozers will arrive at the gates of the Cour de Rome and wipe all trace of it from the face of the earth in a matter of days, the empire of graffiti can only creep further and further over the City in the future. The City authorities have already designated the problem an 'irresistible tide' that the forces of order can hardly monitor let alone effectively control. Day by day the verbal freedom fighters extend the fighting deeper and deeper into the heart of the *beaux quartiers*, further and further into the respectable Metro lines, further and further into the passive nervous systems of millions of slaves. One day it will end by waking them up, the slumbering mass of cannon fodder will wake up to find yelling neologisms in black and red spray paint tattooed across their own noses and the advent of barbaric release, a cathartic cleansing of all their inherited cultural values (the muck and slime that sits at the bottom of their little souls) will be announced. How can we not join the monkey-cries of the fascinated élite, the journalists and professors whose gazes have gone glassy with adoration and worship, and whose tongues are already moving with the grinding rhythms of rap? How can we not feel the excitement of hormonal secretions provoked by this crisis coursing in our veins? If the inalienable premises of this intriguing culture of division, inequality and joyous dissolution is the effortless ability to induce and suffer frenzy, the art of tag is the most solid expression of that premiss. The City is moving according to highly elastic and various rhythms which nevertheless offer a kind of comforting monotony. Drums are beating. The imperial culture feels its rectum contracting with pleasure and anticipation. Wild letters dance across the streets, muscle into private bedrooms, rob grocery stores and nightclubs, flit savagely over bridges and faces and piles of rubble, gang up in loathsome and impractical words that aggress passers by. On all the surfaces of the City, whether horizontal or vertical or neither, the meaningless language of the future is engaged in perpetual carnival, the alphabet's Mardi Gras. As is well known, universal upheavals begin with words on walls and there is no more potent omen of the City's graduation to the status of ramshackle Tower of Babel – a Tower of cultures, of anthropological realities as much as of mumbo-jumbo languages – than the spread of its virile verbal frescoes. One day they will be read and applauded. The unrecognized will be recognized, the intellectuals will paint their faces black and sing hymns to the great divinity of tag and far away, in the mists of aboriginal New York, that distant fatherland whose memory has passed from generation to generation of imported slaves, Afrika Bambataa will turn with gratification in his grave.

145

It will be the end of the long night, mankind's chains will fall away along with the outdated rituals of corporate capitalism, and the City, resplendent in its new garb of outlandish colours and designs – millions of miles of seamless graffitic decoration – will look like a fully mature parakeet killed with a hammer. An unpleasant and snide image perhaps, ladies and gentlemen, but a glorious reality for our children!

The
Gastronome's Dream

Summer has arrived at last with a whiff of plague and pollen and the peasant, with his implacable and unreasonable snobbery, has withdrawn like a snail into a small dark shell which is entirely mental. What disgusts him most about this unbearable season, aside from its blatant flirtation with the aromas of decay, is the deliberate conversion of the nucleus of his beloved City into a kind of dry aquarium for the benefit of thirty-five million visitors whose rollicking, inebriated, plastic faces fill him with the most dandyish and unjustifiable of moral paroxysms. The streets fill with grotesque human curiosities carving peripatetic careers on the pavements of the tourist capital of the Western world. On the first hot nights he roams through Les Halles out of morbid curiosity, not of course to disport himself in the chic terraces of the Café Costes or the Bon Pêcheur, but simply to get a glimpse of the odd knife fight by the Fontaine des Innocentes, especially if the resident CRS get to beat up the offender in complete privacy between two parked meat wagons, or to judge the *artistes* executing their bold and hallucinatory performances: a fire eater in front of the Pêcheur, his skinny chest slimy with petrol, the flares of fire arching like ignited vomit over the spectators' heads; the imitation Popeye with a smashed-up little face crunched over a pipe, a tin can in one hand, who moves with dreamlike slowness through space while a fat man in a straw boater plays an accordion. The tourist zones are heaving and unstable stomachs ingesting vast amounts of pulped material, sharks' bellies filled with human tyres and bones and capable at any minute of reacting violently against their own rapacious *gourmandise*, spitting up bile, burping, rumbling, throwing up or wallowing in hedonistic contentment. The warm atmosphere of early summer brings crowds on to the streets for most of the night. The City at least has none of the

149

morguish dullness of London or Milan. Millions of excitable and blind corpuscles course through its arteries along with the diseases peculiar to human blood, the parasitisms, alcoholisms and intoxications.

While the peasant enters this flowing of blood willingly, it causes him physical anguish to enter the tourist *arrondissements,* the sixth or the second, for example, which – although their indigenous inhabitants might pretend otherwise – are slowly disintegrating under a bacterial wave, a miasmal tide, of virile vulgarity that will not be stopped by little things such as superior sneers and graceful retirement from the scene. No, the tribes of vicious gnomes (the hordes of ululating, tattooed atavars in Viking gear) are here to stay. They deeply appreciate the Coca-Cola sunshades on the rue de Buci and the stench of processed flesh by St Michel. The intestinal streets between Boulevard St Michel and the rue St Jacques have lost for ever their medieval or even their Flaubertian overtones. Rue de la Harpe has dissolved the ghosts of *L'Education sentimentale* and opened its heart to the urban Disneyland, whose paying guests expect much more than facile nostalgia and literary regrets. It is surprising that the entire area has not yet been enveloped in a gigantic film of high-tech plastic like a sealed sandwich in a motorway café and placed under permanent spotlights and electronic surveillance. Just as there has been a 'Disneyland of the Revolution' in the Tuileries for the Bicentennial celebrations, a cardboard leisure park of such phantasmal vulgarity and pointlessness that upper zones of sublimity are unconsciously attained, so the rest of Paris should logically submit to the same treatment. Those ineffable geniuses Hennin and Normier, grandiose architects of the Park of Spectacles designed to commemorate ephemerally the Revolution (everything will be dismantled the following November!), have set the pace for the imperialism of kitsch in the next century. History lives again, neatly telescoped, in these fake guillotines, orators in fancy dress, fluffy 'street girls' showing us the wiles of revolutionary seduction, papier mâché sansculottes, androids delivering fiery jeremiads against monarchy and slavery, period barrel organs, 1789 boxer shorts and videoed decapitations. Why should the same thing not be done everywhere? The principle should at least remain inviolable, whatever variations there are in the application. The only problem is that it cannot be summer all the time, and it is summer that breeds kitsch as a dead body produces ptomaine. As Europeans become voyeurs of their own history, it is only natural that they should become voyeurs of their own cities.

As spring and then summer bring warmer days, the giant belly which is the City – and not just that bohemian part of it formerly located at Les Halles – becomes acidic and bilious with kitsch, so that even crimes take on a hallucinatory quality which mark them off for crimes committed in more temperate times of the year. The pepsins and rennins of this digestive organ – we mean the police, the judiciary and the arbiters of good taste – become somnolent and ineffective against the onset of aestival barbarity. In the Bois de Boulogne, transvestites are found shot in the head – first 'Francine', assassinated on April 5th and then one Pierre Saboni, or 'Clémentine', found with a bullet through the temple at dawn. On the rue de Budapest a tenement is set on fire by underground arsonists and a client, edging his way to safety along a third-floor windowsill after interrupting proceedings with one of the 'Ghanaians', slips and falls to an uncomfortable death, thus engendering a spate of black jokes among the whores. At the same time the Grand Rabbi of France, Joseph Sitruk, sends a telegram of condolence to Father Armogathe, curé of the church of St Pierre de Chaillot after he is wounded by a bomb planted by a mysterious commando group called Gracchus Babeuf Section, sworn enemies of 'Islam, Christianity and Judaism' and all other sects actively engaged in implanting 'fascism' in the heads of the masses. Meanwhile on the rue Dunois in the thirteenth, a seventeen year old is defenestrated in his own apartment block by two thugs of the same age for having refused to hand over his scarf and 200 francs at exactly the same moment as a hotel on the rue Bailly in the third bursts into flames and carbonizes two immigrant workers asleep in their beds. The same Section Gracchus Babeuf running amok in honour of the summer solstice? Incredible bacilli stirred up by the heat, by the release of the fumes of decomposing food and the gases of indigestion? The churning stomach of the City of Food, the Temple of Gastronomy, is certainly capable of releasing a whole gamut of noxious odours into the atmosphere and rising to the head, infiltrating the nervous system and causing assorted migraines, flatulences and attacks of dyspepsia. The peasant who treads so daintily and distastefully through the streets of the summer capital of Europe, who feels his own stomach turning nauseously on its axis and whose malignant nose picks up every tiniest malodour emanating from the bacteriological combustions of the mountains of food that surround him on all sides, is aware – in his morbid and over-sensitive way – of the fraudulence of metaphors. For him the City is not a metaphoric stomach but a real one. The function of eating, the ritual of refined gorging, the processing of millions of tons of produce fills him simultaneously with awe and derision. Of all the cities he has known Paris is the one where the human nose is the most elongated and refined. It is the mouth, lips, tongue, belly and anus of its continent. It is the pearl of gastronomic Shangri Las, boiling in its food lust, barely ceasing to wipe its lips, clean its teeth or inspect its own stools. It is the capital of devouring and the metropolis of sauces. Its secret life is one long, sweetly convulsive bowel movement. It is the great intestine that connects the mouth of a whole civilization to its lightly perfumed rectum. It is the guts and liver of Europe, alive with enzymes and chemical chains. We no longer have the right to talk about the belly of Paris; from now on we will refer to the Paris-belly, the urban liver, the Urinal Tract of Light, the Great Stomach of the White Shark: that which eats and spits out everything under the sun.

The peasant is a dreamer, this is his record. According to our doctors, dreaming is no longer necessary, it can be replaced by waking activities such as bicycling, writing, water-colour painting, callisthenics, cooking or group sex in dimmed and carefully warmed swimming pools. But nevertheless there is one thing he cannot prevent himself from dreaming about, and that is the endless, terrifing fluxion of food.

It's not that he likes gastronomic idylls, expert effusions about *foie gras* and Iranian caviar, or any kind of food journalism for that matter. On the contrary. Along with his *bête noire*, travel writing (*Enlightening Train Odysseys to Ulan Bator and Back, My Favourite Transylvanian Vineyard Reappraised by Donkey*), he hates all forms of peripatetic drooling over exotic places, gorgeous food and neo-colonial hotels. The poetic eye of the experienced and eloquent traveller throws him into spasms of disgust, just as the slippery expertise of scribbling epicureans brings out the forlorn ascetic in him. He would willingly subject all of them to excruciating and ingenious Oriental tortures in order to turn them back into ordinary people. In fact, it is merely sufficient for him now to see an insouciant but perfectly evoked tropical décor in the background, a whiff of Technicolor Third Worldism or off-the-beaten-track parading, for him to fall to his knees foaming at the mouth and begin mashing the carpet with his teeth. The dancing paradises of other worlds leave him stone cold and, worse, terminally suspicious. His dreams of food are not sensual or touristic, they are pathological and inevitable. They are part of the immediate and fascistic reality that subdues and controls him and from which he regards it as pointless to escape. Nor can it be theorized about, for there is nothing to attach thought to and there is nothing to which anything as playful or trivial as an idea could be relative. The matter that presses against his bowels or his ribs is too primitive to be appropriated by any conceivable academicism. It impinges, lightly and mysteriously, presses in upon him and causes him to collapse inwards without the benefit of any kind of compensating idea. He is simply alone with his guts and his toilet bowl. When he imagines dying he imagines it above all as a loss of control over the processing of food, a ludicrous and anti-tragic ataxy of the bowels resulting in embarrassing noises, foul stenches and an inner fluidity, a liquefying of the works.

The structure of the human being, its dignity and godlikeness, lies in the firmness and order of the digestive organs. It lies in control over matter. We are brainwashed into accepting the moralism that nature must never be dominated, but as food is the part of nature we know best and which most intimately affects us, it will have to be admitted once and for all that loss of dominance in the area where human and nature interact with the greatest continuity – that is, in the intestine – is tantamount to reduction in the order of things, to an obliteration of significance. Or do you think that the farcial loss of a specific dignity – as specific to the human genus as an atomic weight is to all the elements – can be suffered with impunity? What if Hamlet farted on stage? What if Adam, father of the race, developed unmistakable symptoms of diarrhoea? What if Medea came down with dysentery? What is disease but the absolutely serene course of nature sodomizing her creations? What is diarrhoea but the cheerful revenge of food upon our so-called gastronomes? Believe us, fellow peasants, food is not an innocent and sweet trifle to be played with, even though it appears to waltz so benignly upon our plates and tables. It is nature herself, stupid, cruel and ruthless. Everything is food, including yourselves, even if it is only bacteria which eat you now. Nature, over which you naturally and melodiously coo and rub your hands, that plump and fertile part-time goddess who manures your unconscious and whose backside you would so dearly like to kiss, that fat cow of a deity whom you vaguely imagine as some tinkling ethnic icon or as a smiling dairymaid covered in gossamer and tentacles of ivy, is no other than the mindless sadist who has commanded all living things to eat all other living things with a perpetual and inane violence, that lobotomized designer who casually exterminates dinosaurs and dodos, sabre-toothed tigers and hairy mammoths, and whose supposed capacity to maintain harmonious order is merely the effect of the relentless whip that ensures continual discontinuity, the stick which flagellates every beast on its path to consumption. Nature, as all true peasants are fully aware, is the greatest advocate of vulgar consumerism the universe has so far produced.

Armed with this foreknowledge the peasant dreams about the things he eats, a dreaming which is incessant, infantile and pseudo-sexual. There is nothing profound in his dreaming. There is nothing witty or perceptive about it, it lurches through his sleeping or waking head with the insolence of all cerebral masturbation. If he wasn't dreaming about food, after all, he would be writing sub-scientific Marxist pamphlets or measuring the flights of birds. He would be as abstracted, self-deluding and irrelevant to the world as any human being could be. He is salvaged by his persistent and frequently dirty oneiric habit.

He opens his dreaming eye, then, and in one glimpse he sees the City laid below him like an Edwardian banquet table laden down with innumerable heart-burning courses separated here and there by bitter sorbets and plates of fruit. The City is a pyramid of food with tiny human insects attached to it, nibbling away at its edges. And immediately, without the slightest prompting from the unconscious, he dreams that he is floating down the rue de Montorgueil equipped with a magical oesophagus and stomach capable of ingesting without limit, a monstrous digestive apparatus appropriate only to dream figures of the order of Pantagruel and Cyrano.

What is it that draws him to the street that winds its way from Les Halles to the rue Réaumur, last diluted fragment of that legendary belly which survives only in the betrayal of literature? Why, of course, the smell of caramelized apples emanating from Stohrer the *pâtissier*. What, in fact, could be more complementary to the aforementioned oneiric habit than the blue and white striped awning, navy blue façade in carved wood and multi-coloured ice-cream trolley posted outside at Stohrer, Parisian *pâtissiers* since 1730? While odour-hunting down the sprawling, noisy, hedonistic rue Montorgueil he cannot stop halting himself on the pavement under the dainty awning and the two windows filled with geraniums above it and peering through the small shop windows into the fantastic turquoise interior that reduces him to the blind and adoring consumerism of his childhood. His eyes go round and glazed. The smell of apples and butter comes out in solid gusts, knocking pedestrians off balance. The windows themselves are divided into sweets and savouries, the former on the left, the latter on the right-hand side of the door. The right-hand side filled with trays of *gigots d'agneau glacés*, *bavarois de crevettes* and tubs of hare terrine, does not interest him. This goes for the right-hand side of the interior as well, despite the opulence of its *feuilletés* and flans. The left-hand side, however, is the proper focus of his sleep-walking: here there is a delirious display of pendant plastic parrots perched on wire seats surrounded by boxes of Stohrer chocolates bearing the same incomprehensible motif. Below them, ranged like their savoury counterparts on plain trays that reveal a charming smack of honest provincialism sit the dreamy pastries, tarts and geometrically severe *gateaux* whose edges are razor sharp and whose colours are simple and pure. Next to these stratified confections constructed like sections of Jurassic soil, with layers of *pâte macaron, mousse praliné* and caramelized nuts packed into dense and formidable cubes with all the gravity of a Japanese picnic, lie casual assortments of macaroons. But it is necessary to venture inside, into the pale Pompeian-First Empire décor of large wall mirrors and delicately painted mouldings, of life-sized frescoes of sweet-eating nereids in fluttering chitons and recumbent bowls of summer fruit set within gold garlands, in order to submit to the narcotic profusion of Stohrer's fantasies.

Here there is nothing of the slick modernism of Peltier or Christian Constant, no lamina of arty professionalism laid over the childish indulgence of stuffing your face with sweets. Stohrer is the house of Hansel and Gretel, the chocolate cottage of the fairytale. Its frills are modest and rooted in the tolerance of other ages. The mirrors produce sparkling but subdued reflections. Above, a turquoise oval ceiling, which should be filled with *trompe l'oeil* scenes of angelic turbulence. Under the glass counters, submerged in the blues, creams and golds that surround them on all sides, sleep the rows of Ali-Babas, *royal menthes, nouméas, noisettines* and *tartes bourdaloues,* along with the *croissants, pains au chocolats* and *napolitains*. A notice outside the shop confronts the casual stroller with a highly scientific graph in which most of the famous bakers of Paris appear acidulously appraised in relation to each other in the matter of making *croissants,* and by means of which we learn that while the *croissants* of Le Fournil de Pierre are grossly shaped, over sugared and in all ways ambiguous, and those of Réné St Ouen thick, supine, mushy and floury in taste, those of Stohrer are perfectly crusty, imbued with a pleasing classical crab form, ungreasy, sufficiently firm in texture and shot through with the correctly light taste of butter. This is indeed a rarity in the heretical City of today. The *pains aux raisins,* too, although the notice does not boast about them, are filled with just the right amount of custard and are cooked to the perfect degree of semi-resistant hardness around the rims. But at this point, as he is perhaps letting his greedy infantile eyes roam lustfully over the arched chocolate back of an Alhambra decorated with brown and cream leaves and truffle berries or the caramelized top of a *puits d'amour* set off against a background of paper lace, and dreaming of rum punch and layers of cream in either, he is rudely not to say catastrophically awakened from his wallowing in the turquoise boudoir of pastry by the incestuous cackling of food dandies all around him, for suddenly he is surrounded and there is no getting away from them. Professors, experts, self-taught men, culinary aesthetes, little Neros of the taste buds, gastronomic pedants, pastriologists, Professors of Higher *Pâtisserie*, dons of the world of flans, PhDs in strawberry tarts, lecturers in *forêts noires*. They have appeared out of nowhere in a swarm, their notebooks are out and already they are arguing, analysing, discoursing, holding forth upon this and that aspect of the sweet tooth's art, a mad circus of bearded gastronomes with moist lips and honeycombed, elongated noses! What a dream it's become, and in the middle of the rue Montorgueil! The peasant holds his hands to his ears but nothing can stop the deluge of masterful comments and observations, of argument and counter-argument, from overwhelming his simple, rustic brain.

'Too insolent, the *royale menthe*, and too prejudiced against the *mousseline de chocolat*. Seven out of ten.'

'Rubbish! Blatant racism!'

'We will have to wait until your notes are published in full. However, we can say with some certainty, not to say . . . well, in short, you're forgetting the origins of the *royale menthe*. The essence, sir, is mint. *Menthe fraiche, si je peux dire* . . . as fresh as possible *et tutti frutti*!'

'*Tutti frutti*! The analysis holds!'

'What you say, sir, about the *menthe fraiche* in the *royale menthe* may be true, but how can you explain the overbearing arrogance, the injudicious injudiciousness, the tone . . . *pimpante et rageuse, que peux-je dire?* . . . of the *punché au rhum léger* in the Alhambra, not to mention the sheer iconoclasm of the *chocolat amer* in the Criollo? Do we not detect a note of false values? Six out of ten for the Criollo and five for the Alhambra!'

'Liberal fags!'

'*A priori! In grosso modo!*'

'Honorary election for the *mousse de fruits cassis*!'

'An evident and inexcusable bias towards pears . . . *tutti frutti* revisionism . . . dignity for *charlottes* . . . a re-examination of *péchés mignons* . . . a radical and uncompromising re-evaluation of the entire hierarchial system of *bonbons,* tarts and *crèmes caramels* . . . absence of ethnocentricity in the matter of the three Pyramids . . .'

'The Pyramids are African!'

'*A posteriori* and QED . . .'

'Honorary election for the Three Pyramids!'

Yes, it's true, Stohrer manufactures three different types of pyramidal confection, one of dark brown chocolate (*le Kheops*), one white (*le Khephren*) and one coffee (*le Mykerinos*). The City's pseudo-Masonic, revolutionary Egyptian imagery lives on even here, perpetuating the charming but fraudulent fantasies of Nilotic omniscience. And since our academics are mesmerized by questions of ethnic and cultural displacement, they go into paroxysms over the Three Pyramids (not to mention, of course, the Ali-Baba, the *nouméa* and the *criollo*), so much so that the peasant, momentarily drowned in their lecherous discourses, finds himself drifting away from them, sucked back into the rue Montorgueil and away from the blue and cream shimmer of Stohrer. But it is not only his old-fashioned and reactionary tastes that expel him from their company, it is also the pungent smell of fish coming from the other side of the street. The tumult of this artery, given over almost entirely to the delirium of food, sacks and pillages his frontal lobes, rendering them entirely subjective. He waddles past the butchers' shops at the end of the street where it debouches by St Eustache and the alien reflective pavilions of the Forum des Halles (the glittering eggs of some pterodactyl of the unpleasant future) and goes in and out of the aisles of hanging rabbits, their livers dangling from carved-up underbellies by tiny webs of fat, the thickets of pheasants, capons and moorhens, the enslaved piles of trussed-up ducklings and corn-fed chickens, the bowls of tripe and *boudin noir, tournedos* and blanched tongues, arrays of nutty brains and under-estimated ears, trotters and jellies, horse steaks and sides of boar. He is an omnivorous customer. Like the shoppers of the neighbourhood he flinches before nothing, and this can be liberally interpreted, as it always is, as a calm and wholesome acceptance of the diversity of nature, a refusal to be squeamishly selective when confronted with its awful riches. The proletarian opulence of the Montorgueil butchers is reflected in the tumbling crushed-ice displays of the two major fishmongers, especially the bigger of the two at no. 62. The smells from here have dragged him away from the Stohrer boudoir, after all, causing him to ignore in passing the honourable Enard next door, and that in spite of their superbly vulgar enamelled chandeliers. The *poissonnière*, on the other hand, reminds him of the cascading crustaceans of the rue Lepic which he visits scrupulously every day, if only to 'window-lick' and which successfully populate his waking dreams with impossibly armoured submarine edibles, green and morose sea snails and the tragic lobsters whose enigmatic and incessantly active pincers denote the value they place upon their own lives.

The Montorgueil shop, on the other hand, surpasses even those delectable emporia of living gastronomic corpses of the deep. It is deeper inside, or at least seems so due to the size and seriousness of its theatrical displays: the banks of ice containing hundreds of marine species swirled around decorative boulders, fishermen's baskets, palm fronds, clusters of enormous fresh irises, fir twigs, lemons and bales of rosemary. Through this artificial but convincing sea-landscape in which the 'water' has been arrested in the form of that fine and granular ice that so elicits our admiration, the confused eye, scrambling among the diverse medley of mineral and animal forms, comes across arched red snappers in the act of jumping, whorled skinned eels roped around rocks, salmon sliced into steaks and reconstituted into their original languid shapes while their mouths protrude into the street. John Dorys, rainbow trout and fleshy whitings mate against a dazzling backdrop of crystals while sea slugs, crayfish and scallops slide in and out of nooks and crevices, pile themselves up like mounds of heads under the powerful lamps that make them glitter. Shoals of mackerel and sprat weaving through the exotically unmarine vegetation, ambushes of squid and fillets of shark, pike and sword fish, grey shrimps and sombre colonies of sleeping crabs, everything edible in the oceans dredged up from the sea floors and brought into the cruel and crystalline light of the store where electricity and ice combust together to recreate the palatial interiors of the Snow Queen. The bodies of these prostrate organisms, given a paradoxical and titillating glory by their exposure among these miniature symbolic landscapes, are cold and diamantine: the cold they give off hits the lungs and makes the peasant recoil at the thought of graves.

The store is organized as a refined and sensual bordello of marine food. Unlike the Spartan and ludicrously plain emptiness of English fishmongers, where it is a struggle to see anything interesting and which deliberately militates against the immoral enjoyment of carnivorous activities and aesthetic stimulations (it is surprising that the dour trays of limited produce aren't covered with mourning shrouds), the Parisian fish shop exults in visual whorishness, flourishes its catholicity of taste and deliberately takes upon itself the glory of biological diversity. Even the little tubs of seaweed cavort with the consumer. Even the cashier, enthroned at the back of the shop in an open kiosk bedecked with herbs and citrus fruits, flirts with the unsatisfied and salacious hunger of the eaters of fish. She could be a mermaid for all the awed shoppers know – a sympathetic sister of the cavalcades of oceanic animals that surround her. She wears a knowing and lascivious smile. Her eyes are green and correspond in unforeseen ways with the speckled and mucal spines, glazed black eyes, tinted underbellies and motionless fins. The galoshes and blue overalls of the men do not concern or in any way compliment her. She is the Alice Ozy of the aquatic cornucopia, inspirer of delicate fish soups, haughty *soles Bercys* and fatal *bouillabaisses*. In her eyes are printed the boredom and spiralling sensuality of the trade in flesh.

She reminds the peasant of the magnificent woman who stands behind the counter at the Compagnie Coloniale de Thé on the rue Lepic, in her two-tone tan shoes, transparent specs, Walkyrie chignon and perfect red mouth, majestic and hyper-sexual guardian of the orange and strawberry teas, lime infusions and tin Lipton boxes emblazoned with courtly Chinese scenes. The two woman are identical in their relation to their produce. Like the cashier at no. 62, the busy *patronne* of the Compagnie Coloniale is surrounded – if you peer in at her from the outside – by verdant clumps of bamboo and bric-à-brac symbolically or practically related to the purveying of tea and coffee: percolators, odd little grinders and other esoteric appurtenances, the lovely round green boxes of Yunnan tea, packets of cinnamon and lemon grass, pepper pots and wicker filters. Like the mermaid her lower half is often not revealed and she floats seductively and maternally among her fragrant charges, a Renoir bar-girl in front of a mirror – no, how revolting! – a *diva* of tea whose hair you imagine as being lightly scented with bergamot, whose unparalleled, mature cleavage, if you were so lucky as to be able to bury your childish face in it, you find to be musky, smoky, pungent with the dry perfume of Lapsang Suchong.

Why is it always women who fill these dangerous and ambivalent posts, who act as the agents of the elective affinities that draw us to the eating of food? It is best, or worst, in the *crémeries*. Yes, in the intense cheese and dairy produce shops – those specialist stores of genius which are the paramount glory of Paris – you will find the presence of women behind the counter most volcanic, deranging and intoxicating. There is something in the textures of curdled and processed milk that reacts alchemically with their flesh and their hormones to turn them into minor cheesy goddesses fully equipped with atavistic charms and bodily attributes which in turn make their *chèvres, vacherins, crèmes fraiches* and St Aulbrays insidiously and alarmingly irresistible. They know they do it, too. They are never the first to wipe those knowing smiles off their faces. Their cheeks are pale and waxy, chilled along with everything else, but out of the background of pale yellows, creams and lactic whites their lips stand out brilliantly, as do the chocolate and cyan centres of their eyes. As the peasant makes his way up the rue de Montorgueil in the direction of the rue des Petits Carreaux, the rue Réaumur and the green lattice gate that announces the realm of food, he is more and more distracted by these tutelary deities ensconsced in their altars of titbits. And not only the dairymaids, but the Rubensesque women who thrive in the moist darkness and secrecy of the *charcuteries*, whose secondary sexual features derive potency from the proliferation all around them of mounds of *oeufs en gelée, coquilles au crabe, bouches de reine*, puffy gnocchi, gelled rabbits surmounted by glazed nuts, heavily minted *tabbouleh*, Baltic herrings, *foie gras de canard, croustades au thons, pamplemousses exotiques* in a *sauce cocktail*, bundles of asparagus in *sauce mousseline*, artichokes with *crevettes, grenadin de veau* in pineapple and eclectic bales of *blinis, mille feuilles*, stuffed mussels, *brioches au roquefort* and chestnut flans. In the unreal interior of the *traiteur*, buried in the most highly organized and rarefied chemistries of food on earth, all human beings take on the look of the clients and 'servers' of the near-by rue St Denis, and we would even go so far as to claim this as a compliment.

The peasant, ambling in his primitive way up the rue Montorgueil, stopping for a marc at La Grappe d'Orgueil, avoiding scrupulously the rundown offices of the Parti Socialiste in case he is accidentally recognized by someone, feeling, it is true, tempestuous inflations afflict him in his reproductive zones, appears to be convinced only that women are essentially treated in the same way as food, consumed, tasted, ingested, swallowed, burped up, expelled in the form of faeces – but suddenly interrupting his dream in order to recoil with revulsion from such crude, pseudo-liberal, sub-feminist meditations (which are truly not worthy of the complexity of the subject and which, to speak frankly, he considers not without a certain amount of sadistic intrigue), he finds himself before he knows it standing aimlessly, like a stranded gastronomic angel, on the pavement of the rue Réaumur with a taste of cheese in his mouth. Let's face it, he thinks to himself literally dreamily, we live not in the City of Food but in the City of Women. The supermarket will divorce cheese from plunging *décolletées*, plastic wrapping will keep bananas and erections apart, people will see through all this childish and anachronistic erotic flim-flam, they will think about vitamin value, fibre content, waistlines and love handles, iron levels and quotas of trace elements. The presence of selenium or zinc will weigh more with the conscientious consumer than the corny poetry of dairymaids and cherry-like nipples. You will serve yourself without the inconvenient intermediary of winks, half-smiles, flirtatious games or the possibility of secret rendezvous with food nymphs smelling, even in the back row of the cinema, of fresh artichokes, smoked cheeses and *saucisson sec*. The desensualization of food is perfectly inevitable. The English example will be universally followed. The rue Montorgueil will have to go, of course . . . for one thing, it's unhygienic, it swarms with microbes and lethal doses of listeria. The dream of food ends with nostalgic onanism in the dark. It is time to pinch yourselves and assure a speedy and healthy return to reality. The glory and exhilaration of the sexless supermarket awaits you, and it is even a curious fact that the peasant himself has no hesitation in looking forward to it. But before he goes shopping at the gigantic temple of functional food at the Carrefour shopping centre, he is resolved to indulge himself in another dream altogether: the dream of the City of Women, for this City at least has an endless and verifiable future. The City of Women is all around us and recently, quite independently from the metaphors of food and consumption, it has made an impressive transformation from slave state to monarchy to fledgling republic. The City of Women is the only part of the present that will exist in the future without uncertainty. It is the seed of future meteoric storms.

Thus confronted with the imminent end of his dream, the gastronome-peasant decides to pinch himself hard and, taking his nose between his index finger and his thumb, proceeds to do so in order to wake up. For a moment he blacks out and then, as always happens, he blinks his eyes as he emerges from his state of sleep. Yes, the severe pinch makes him wake up. But what is his surprise when he finds that, instead of cosily ensconced in a warm bed surrounded by a pleasantly aired and darkened room, he is still standing lost and disappointed, at the corner of the rue Réaumur and the rue Montorgueil, at the miserable edge of his own banished dream?

City of Women

It is necessary to recognize facts: the world is changing for the better. The impetus of change is irreversible. The radical will is pulling the strings from behind the scenes like a dome-foreheaded, high-thinking master puppeteer. Yes, change is in the air. In a back page of the *New York Review of Books* the peasant is reassured of the greater goodness which is coming – it's just around the corner – by a large advertisement for an upside-down atlas with the logo: For a Kinder, Gentler America. The priests of goodness have suddenly realized – and with what penetrating perception – that – 'on top', 'above' and 'over', even expressed graphically as in the cartographical representation of nations as they actually appear from space, equal nothing less than notions such as 'superior', 'nicer' and 'much better'. In other words, 'Northern'. How catastrophic! An immediate and radical solution is immediately called for. Why, what could be easier – simply turn the map upside down! Now, for a certain sum and the correct postage included, your business, office or school can see the world for what it is, or at least for what it could be, or even will be when the forces of goodness have demonstrated to a benighted and arrogant world-dominating élite the vicious error of their ways. The confused viewer, obviously tainted by the cultural bad habits of a lifetime of crass indoctrination, now peruses a wholly revised, refreshed and re-invented world, a paradise of moral re-adjustment, in which Guatemala is 'higher up' (i.e. closer to where the North Pole, the insidious indicator of historical worth, used to be situated) than Canada, in which Burundi is 'above' West Germany and formerly insignificant Belize is 'over' the almighty United States. It is not clear from the small-scale illustration of this completely surrealist map whether the place names are printed upside down as well, so forcing upon the unwary user the necessity of inducing insupportable cramps in the neck, and nor is it clear how long-distance travel is to be organized or the migratory patterns of birds explained. None of this matters. What is important is the salutary shock to the global order. Goodness, fellow citizens, is increasing and before long it will run quietly in your veins, it will inoculate and intoxicate you. It will make your eyes shine like idealistic Roman candles. The iron penicillin of goodness will soon cleanse the bloodstream and organs such as the heart and the liver from within. *The Upside-Down Map of the World* will seem perfectly natural and the banal interjections of reality will seem as irrelevant as the heckling of a South American *generalissimo* at a Sri Chimnoy Divine Light convention. To your flutes, citizens, and open up your hearts and minds to the shafts of light of the future!

In the disappointing Turkish toilet of the present, however, we have to content ourselves with compromises. We are aware that the world is going down the plug-hole of the sink of nightmares, and that despite the heroic rearguard action of the martyrs of Action Directe, the beautiful national ideals of Switzerland and Scandinavia, the anti-vivisection militants of Inserm and the upright warnings of Arlette Laguiller posted on walls all over the City. Nor have we forgotten the humble and anonymous gestures of the college students ducking Contra bullets in the cotton fields of Nicaragua. But at least there is one glimmer of hope, a spark on the horizon. That glow on the edge of our field of vision is the City of Women. The City of Women is being built in the shambles of the present disaster and the citizens of this new metropolis are already blowing their seductive trumpets. The future is coming home to roost in the present in the form of mobilized cohorts of goodness dressed as Amazons. With the benefit of having had their left breasts lopped off in order to enable them to shoot straighter, they fire off their deadly salvoes of arrows left, right and centre.

You should have seen it coming.

You should have been better prepared.

But then, you should never have been a collaborator in the first place. You should have learned a lesson from *The Upside-Down Map of the World*.

No city has been more feminized than Paris, more effectively moulded to the contours of the female myth. It is the only one to have seen a particular culture of prostitution, even an architecture of the courtesan, an architecture whose apotheosis is the Hotel Paiva. The Paris of the Second Empire was a satrapy of the courtesan, not only as the West's first society to be dominated by the cult of woman, but also as the first in which the self-made woman, the prostitute-capitalist, was a formidable controller of blocks of shares in South American railways and nickel mines in Noumea. For the first time the sex-fantasy puppet persisting aimlessly through history is able to turn the tables on the society that breeds and tames her. The first empress of the City of Women is a whore, Thérèse Lachmann, La Marquisa de Paiva and later Countess Henckel von Donnesmarck, the daughter of a weaver in the foreign ghetto in Moscow, anthrophage and female vampire, consumer of aristocrats and agent of social cancer: the richest prostitute in human history and the builder and owner of the most expensive house – in relative terms – ever constructed in the City. The most terrifying incarnation of the will to power and money of the nineteenth century is a sex goddess actively laying the foundations of the worship machine of Hollywood. For the Parisian prostitute is the foundation of all female screen idols of the twentieth century. Marie Duplessis, the Dame aux Camélias, emerges a century later, both figuratively and literally, as Greta Garbo.

What is the essential ingredient of this manifestation of the self-legitimizing Woman, whose first letter must from now on be made a capital letter? Duplessis was consumptive, volatile, intellectual and doomed. She died at the age of twenty-three. Liszt was obsessed by her. Verdi erected *La Traviata* over her tomb. The perfectly realized Romantic life: provincial origins, debauched father, early exploitation, prostitution followed by One True Love and death from consumption. In her apartment opposite the Madeleine, bought for her by Baron de Stackelberg, the creditors dismantled the curtains as the last rites were administered – the arc of a tiny adolescent's life continuing the poetic tradition. On the other hand, most of the courtesans lived to be pathetic, grasping old women ensconced in obscure hotels among the relics of their exploded glory. They published their memoirs and died in agony, like everyone else, of cancer of the intestines or infarctions of the myocardium. Most were like La Barucci or Esther Guimond: spiritually raped early in life, denuded of indispensable illusions of sexual romance, sexual Machiavellians with a nose for blackmail and politics, flies around the heads of powerful men, amassers of fortunes they could not control. They erected an alternative society in which the phosphorescent flow of millions of francs attracted an alternative intelligentsia. Some, like Mogador, ended up as desperate repentants trying to re-enter the society from which they had originally been expelled against their will by means of nunnish abstinence, devotion to duty and the funding of charities. Some, like Appolonie Sabatier and Blanche d'Antigny, became the contents of books and statues and pieces of music. Sabatier, Baudelaire's Venus, Clésinger's Woman Bitten by a Serpent, Blanche d'Antigny, the immortal Nana. With the exception of Sabatier, what runs through all of their lives is the possibility opened up by the entry on to the stage of history of a volcanic society energized from within by an uncontrollable, brilliant and poisonous pool of capital. The image of Woman is subverted and then re-invented. The prostitute, only vessel of extra-marital desire and financial-erotic fantasy, ceases to be marginal and throws up in her society's face. She swallows cash in addition to semen. She lunches on her own at the Café Anglais or Tortoni's. She drives a brougham in the Bois. She dies of either addiction or a broken heart. She dances at the Bal Bullier, sometimes on the tables, and polkas at the Ranelagh. She plays muse. She invests in nickel mines. She poses for geniuses with long hair. She has affairs with Jewish bankers. She infiltrates the Cents Guards, the Union Club and the imperial family. She moves millions of francs with a sneeze. She formulates foreign policy with a twist of the thighs. And above all she lives in and builds palaces.

The Hotel Paiva recedes from the Champs-Elysées a few paces from the Rond Point and the sculptural foam of the Grand Palais and its accompanying setpieces. It is different from everything around it. The Saudi banks and airline offices which have replaced the neo-Pompeian villas and Gothic castles that once stood in the truly Elysian Fields of the early nineteenth century are unable to outstare its cold arrogance. A fussy but still severe Second Empire façade decorated like an elaborate and haughty pudding with eclectic and fickle odds and ends, classical pilasters, an ornate balcony strewn with thick arabesques, lions' heads launching themselves uselessly into space. Rusticated Renaissance stonework near ground level gives hints of the Palazzo Pitti, the ornate walls on three sides enclose a space now filled with the *bureau de change* in the gay cosmopolitan airport style attached to the Travellers' Club which occupies the hotel, the sleek doors are embossed with polished bronze Grecian busts, endless scrolls, leaves, weaving and poutings in stone, a symphony of mellifluous architectural clichés dancing together in space like the careful make up of a glamorous, well-educated but tarty corpse. It is a frozen building, as frozen in time and space as the corpse of its creator herself, that La Paiva whose last husband, the Count von Donnesmarck, had her pickled in a giant bottle in his German castle and locked in a room for thirty years until a younger wife discovered her at last, as persistent in death as she had been in life.

How many mashers of distinction have climbed the small flight of stairs to the hallway covered with a stuccoed barrel vault where today (a small touch of utilitarian vulgarity) there hangs an over-ordinary thermometer and then proceeded to the claustrophobic interior, where the cool and assurance of massive slabs of masonry induce a mild bout of intimidation? The staircase that rises to the first floor was a legend of nineteenth-century Paris. Made of solid onyx, it cost Paiva over a million francs alone. The colossal bronze lamp-holder that stood at its base has been removed, as have the luxury carpets. Today it feels like a severe Michelangelo tomb. The frescoes of Baudry upstairs remain and the pendulous chandeliers and the ubiquitously oppressive atmosphere of unimaginable flows of cash . . . but in other respects it is a shell, a ruin to the memory of the empire of prostitution which would probably have liked to be romantic but which instead expresses more than anything the desperate desire to be integrated, the longing of the outcast for honour. The craving of the prostitute for adoration finds its way into an architectural language of pomposity and domination. Observing the onyx staircase that was the seventh wonder of the Industrial Age, a calamitous escalator towards operatic seduction on a one and a half ton mahogany bed in the form of a sea chariot, the dramatist Augier remarked: 'Ainsi que la vertu, le vice a ses dégrés.' The over-worked imperial conventions have acquired with time a poignant nostalgia and sadness, however, a nostalgia which could never have been intended. The abrupt destruction of that world by history's first mechanized war has left its monuments stranded in a time vacuum, as distant from the airline offices and aluminium banks as the stubs of Roman columns in a cornfield or the heads of decapitated pharaohs lost in the antiseptic calm of twentieth-century museums. Its lecherous froth has frozen into a spurious but inoffensive pathos as the stone has turned grey and the metal oxidized. And unlike the histrionic monuments imposed upon the City from above by the very society which rejected and despised La Paiva, her hotel at least is submerged in the more interesting mysteries of secretive individual lives lived out in a stupendous and impossible décor of oneiric kitsch which can only force our admiration.

Designed as revenge against those blind to the legitimacy of mercenary sex, as hysterical statement of will to power, self-establishment and self-sublimation in the objective and hard medium of stone, Pierre Mauguin's design, which rose into the air of the summer of 1856, remains as the first entirely female building of the modern age. It is a huge marble vagina thrust defiantly into a landscape of walking phalluses. It is the beginning of the alternative landscape of the paradaisical and nightmarish City of Women . . .

The décor of the Hotel Paiva could well have inspired others in the imaginary female metropolis. In Fellini's *Città delle Donne*, for example, both the Hotel Marmaris, where the Feminist Tribunal convenes, and the villa of the grotesque sexual athlete Cazzone share its atmosphere of unease. It could be said, in fact, that only Fellini has concretely entered the turbulent sector of the imagination where unspeakable slaveries, abortions and rapes occur, the sector which he has called the City of Women and which witnesses the final *regressum ad uterum* of the male under the influence of the imperialism of the female as she exists in his imagination. In *Città delle Donne,* the Don Juanish hero, Snaporaz, reminiscing after dinner, traverses all the grotesque landscapes of his lust, suffering various humiliations on the way. Finally he is invited to stroll through Cazzone's Hall of Fame, in which the monster's conquests are remembered by means of illumined photographs set into the walls and recordings of their moans of pleasure activated by a simple push of a button. He pauses in front of one of them, a pulpy brunette biting on a biscuit: the frozen-food woman stored safely in the male memory bank. But here as elsewhere the feminist terrorist brigades burst in, semi-automatics in hand, and – by one of those disastrous reversals that characterize the liquid world of dreams – the hunter becomes the hunted. The City of Women turns out to be the Stalinist homeland of the disenfranchised feminist masses.

But what chance is there of this happening in Paris?

On the walls of the Metro, the divinities of the City are omnipresent. The Printemps girls are the exact opposite of Fellini's Amazons, since they have turned themselves into sartorial chameleons in search of a constantly elusive sex appeal. Women have become themes. All fashion is a choosing and mixing of themes and every woman must assemble herself coherently as a theme: one day I'm a sailor and the next I'm a sugar-cane hacker in the colonial tropics, and the day after that it's either apartheid or one-breasted astronauts. For the Expo Tropiques: an elastic amphibian in ethnic bikini thigh deep in water holding upright a palm frond that arches back over her head. 'Tous les objets de tous les paradis . . .' We see that it's Tahiti Week just as next week it will be Yak Week and the week after that Snorkelling Week and so on around the year, the *montage* of styles pillaging the world's tribes, utensils, vegetations and landscapes . . . for today, as the happy liberals of Benetton will tell you, the world is a seamless garment woven of many colours that are united.

Yet at the same time it is also evident that a growing predatory boldness is emerging among the technicolour ad-nymphs. Never mind the Printemps windows themselves, which are content with a disappointing sobriety and where a frigid plastic bride in white lace sits paralysed among a pile of Chabanne silverware and Bernadaud plates with her fingers in a Buddhistic sign . . . look around you and you will see that women are becoming more and more naked, increasingly denuded, in exact proportion to the increasing perfection of their skin. They're lounging, flirting, sniggering. They're turning predatory, if you'll be so good as to look at the incontrovertible evidence. And as they become more predatory, their bodies become thinner, more agile and irreproachable. A law of evolution is in effect.

In the safety of a darkened cinema, for example, one of these predatory specimens finds herself eating a well-known commercial yogurt in a hammam (impossible and shameless fantasy!). She is surrounded by oiled and massively muscular male fodder. So much the better: she's wearing only a towel herself. She walks slowly among the pillars and raised daises and she sees paraded in front of her all the possibilities of maleness, bald ones, stout ones, mesomorphs and endomorphs, bicep boys and thigh specialists, Latin ones and Nordic ones. They're all disporting themselves around her. She has only to push a mental button and the specimen of her choice will come bounding over through the steam and catapult her semi-forcibly into a catatonic state of multiple orgasm. Finally she sits by a sweating column and as she dips her spoon into her plastic pot of blueberry yogurt (it's the sign – the incredible effect our active-ingredient blueberry yogurt has on weight-trained young men!) a strapping beast barely covered with a sticky loin-cloth rises and swivels round, ready, we are to suppose (for the film abruptly closes on this provocative shot) to perform the sexual equivalent of one of Hamid's expert and pleasantly excruciating massages.

We are forced, however distasteful we might find it, to acknowledge the right of women to hunt for prey in the privacy of their own dreams. And at the same time we are also forced to acknowledge the existence of whole tribes of these male accessories earning a lucrative living from their bodies, keeping themselves in a perpetual state of muscular readiness and covering their counterparts in real life with shame . . . the shame of not having what the female spectator wants. The City of Women, if this is a foretaste of it, reproduces the tactics of the former City of Men, inverting its strategies, appropriating its weapons. Like a multi-headed armadillo, it storms the bastions of stereotype and turn itself into a perfect replica of that which it has replaced.

Naturally, you will object sarcastically, this is worse than naïve. The inexorable perfecting of women is part of another conspiracy altogether. And aren't women expected to be beautiful according to a sinister and uncontrollable canon? Whatever is admitted, one thing is certain: in Paris, the potential or partial City of Women, a hysteria for perfection is in place. Women are not just objects; they are pieces of movable geometry.

The magazines now are filled with the tools of this geometry. Slimming vectors, fat-blasting creams, aromatic mucopolysaccharides, algae, clays and extracts of green-lipped mussels. The faces of this glorious revolution are already in the air. They are nourished with Arkofluide rich in linolenic gamma acid taken easily in gel-pill form and sold in pharmacies in order to encourage the civic duty of women to improve their inner beauty. Their mouths are only slightly open and inside them can be seen tantalizing vistas of moist teeth honed on the sweet flesh of millionaires. Thinness centres multiply. Anti-wrinkle therapies fall from the sky. Hypoglucidic jams appear on bits of Scandinavian crackers which cocoa-coloured savages in swimsuits hold up to the sun with the gravity of alchemists in the presence of the Philosopher's Stone. Gerbiol Laboratories bring out the fabulous Konjax pill to halve the volume of your thighs, a new programme called Five Kilos Before Summer delivers sexual success on the beaches, and ingenious derivations of ocean products, from iodine and spirulina to seaweeds and Mexican algae, erupt into the light of day. There is aerodynamic improvement all round. It is a delight to the eye. And look at their levels of hygiene – a complete transformation. They smell more pleasant, impregnated as they are with mysterious molecules derived from the souls of flowers.

The male model Tanel, who poses in matador hats and Dim underwear and carries around with him the name of an Armenian blossom, declares that the male mannequin is no longer merely a beautiful object: he tells a story. So it is with women, who have all taken on the flexible aura of animated photographs. They tell a story and so cease being mere objects. Inès de la Fressange, caryatid of Chanel, turns herself from apheta to contessa in the blink of an eye. I tell a story, I am a story, I de-banalize myself.

'Aujourd'hui tu marches dans Paris les femmes sont ensanglantées.'

Their lips above all deserve the above description, they look as if they have been slyly ripped by someone's else's teeth. There is no more ritual and taboo concerning menstruation. The women are not herded away into separate huts while the moon is full.

They have taken fate in their stride. They have mastered their bodies with the aid of Phas Auto-Bronzage and the Babybliss Bodyform.

Over the City, shining even at night, you see the giant faces of sleeping beauties, skin-care deities and keep-fit imps made luminous by the chemical dynamism of Hydra Swiss with Caviar Extracts. Their teeth flash by in the Metro tunnels. No doubt their hearts are beating though you cannot hear them. They fill you with the gas of lust. You are bowled over with admiration. You know they are the shape of bodies and faces to come as the human race fulfils its physiological destiny and becomes – without the slightest irony or retreat – ever more like the image of God.

Often, the peasant imagines himself strolling down his own Hall of Fame modelled on Cazzone's. He pushes a button and is transported instantly back to his own youth. His head swells, he feels fine. They're all under control. He is a little boy with his cork boards of pinned beetles. But at the back of his mind he knows perfectly well that as soon as he is feeling at his ease there will be a bang on the door, a tinkling of smashed glass and they will be here. Ten commandos in battle fatigues and sunshades will burst into his Hall of Fame throwing grenades left and right, firing off their M16s in all directions and shouting the unbearable slogans of female-proletarian insurrection! And instantly he will realize that he is contaminated by the sins of his sex. He is the enemy. He is a rat.

They will rough him up no doubt and knock him to the floor (though as he goes down bleeding he will still notice the hems of white thigh above their stockings). Perhaps, stirred by some ancestral chauvinism, he will drag himself to his knees and repeat Cazzone's anthem to Chauvinist Piggery:

Grande fianchi
Carnosi e bianchi . . .

And so, singing the praises of large and carnal white thighs, he will go down under a hail of blows and thus awake into the grey light of dawn with the inner certainty that his days are indeed numbered in real life, for the City of Women, when it arrives, will put him on trial and send him to a penal colony for ideological reprogramming.

As *The Upside-Down Map of the World* has predicted, the world will be turned on its head and the City will be populated only by female marines, hysterectomied judges and millions of servile tongueless eunuchs. The 100,000 whores of the *fin de siècle* will be an incredible folk memory and emasculated males will be set up on pedestals, upon which they will be simultaneously adored and pelted with rotten eggs. And at the filthy bottom of the nights of the future, desire will probably hatch its unpredictable eggs only under full moons, in harmony with the sacrosanct menstrual cycle. Peasants will have become a ludicrous anachronism. Coins will bear the heads of female presidents in Phrygian caps and loudspeakers from every corner will proclaim the dangers of unspaded boys.

And the planet?

A protected and nourished planet will be nurtured by earth mothers armed with large udders and spinning wheels. The globe will fraternalize happily with the solar system and everything else in space and *The Upside-Down Map of the World* will hang in every bedroom, office and train. Think about it, heirs to our disabused present: you have everything to be grateful for!

But in a dark corner of that same present, inside the even darker hole of his brain, the peasant is stubbornly filled with only one thought as he slumbers through his stuffy microscopic life. It rumbles in the hollows and troughs of his dormant dreaming organ with the force of dyspeptic gurgles crying out in a spirit of cave-man rebellion: women of the wretched earth, I am a weight-lifting poet and I WANT TO SCREW YOU ALL!

The Weight-Lifting Poet

✢

On his interminable peregrinations on foot around the world's most literary city the peasant, who is also, as explained, a weight-lifting poet, is filled with an impossible longing to be immortal. With this melancholy desire in mind he often wanders across the Place Pigalle and, a mere few hundred yards from his home, immerses himself in the nostalgic and half-forgotten Avenue Frochot. This becalmed zone, lost in the last century, could also be called a part of the City of Women since it was the hub of the Bréda, the original Bohemia of the 1840s, the quarter of budding courtesans, the corner of the metropolis where the osmosis of·sex and labourers of art was at its most intense. In the adjoining street, the rue Frochot, the declining thoroughfare where an overspill of Pigalle hostess bars counterfeits the sexuality of a past age without inheriting its wit, Appolonie Sabatier lived at no. 4 at the expense of the Belgian industrialist Mosselman and prepared herself for Baudelaire. In the avenue itself, a hilly, pastoral path of cobbles, gas lamps and luxurious tropical gardens, Alice Ozy visited at night the studio of the painter Chassérieu who turned her into the 'Baigneuse Endormie'. Plaques pinned to the secretive and exotic array of Venetian villas, ochre Gothic fantasies and eccentric cottages, dormant behind crumbling gate posts and bales of ivy and St John's wort, record the passing of Paul Mercourt the marine painter, Eugène Brieux the dramatic author and Victor Massé; but it is the ghosts of Berlioz, Gerard de Nerval, Victor Hugo, Delacroix and Théophile Gautier who assemble in this silent hollow barred at both ends to traffic and guarded at the rue Victor Massé end by a guardian mysteriously lodged in a beamed, Tudor-style lodge. The surface of the road is cracked and broken up. In the depths of the fantastical gardens birds let out a spiralling music. No other sound penetrates here.

It is a Pompeian street arrested not by a downpour of ash but by the departure of the denizens of Murger's *Bohème* created within its walls. The City's most beautiful street has taken a whiff of opium and fallen asleep, the Place Bréda has been wiped off the map, Dinochau's has disappeared and the weirdly exuberant vegetation of its secret gardens explodes slowly upwards and outwards, gently engulfing its memories in the calm green of chlorophyll.

Along with this evacuation of the Bréda, this gradual extermination of bohemians, the race of poets themselves have turned into subterranean rats scuttling along the City's hidden sewers and obscure margins, as obsolete as the courtesans who once served as their umbilical cords. Feeling like a gathering tempest of a late afternoon lust the need to commit to paper some dastardly act of loghorrhoeic passion, the peasant hurries like a criminal down the rue Henri Monnier and plunges into the Café Ali half-way down on the left, where he is in the habit of taking his hookah with a fine wad of pure Egyptian *chichi* at thirty-five francs a go. And here, sprawling awkwardly on one of the cushions and revelling in a strangely subversive décor of orange light and travel posters while filling his belly with small Arab pastries, he composes in his head whole epic poems in perfectly rhyming hexameters which, by the time he has rushed home and taken out the typewriter, he has utterly forgotten . . . for it is the *chichi* which gets him going and there is nothing to replace it except perhaps a mouthful of narcotic kola nuts. He realizes that in the Homeric age of sublime orality he would have been better employed as a wrestler, ship-builder or public executioner. He is a poet by accident. Besides, aren't poets a kind of rat species today, endlessly scuttling along hidden sewage pipes and though underground grottoes, embarrassing and boring entities whose metrical effusions give rise only to perfectly oval yawns? The poet has become a rat, both spiritually and – more importantly – physically. The problem with rats is that they breed.

Paris is the most literary of cities. The sixth *arrondissement* is the site of the world's most civilized and sophisticated literary life. It is sweet, calm and honey-coloured. The stone of the buildings complements the intellectual honey that flows through its minds. Sweetness, light and the tinkle of glasses. Books are consumed here in the way that other nations use finely scented toilet paper. There is no ignorance. There is no vulgarity. There is no abrasion. There are no loud voices. The eyes are liquid with peaceful intelligence and tolerance. And above all the rats are able to peep their heads above ground, through the manholes as it were, without shame or fear. They can blink in the light of day, which they must otherwise shun and flee lest they be discovered by the police or by over-inquisitive passers by and look around at a landscape wholly hospitable to their innermost needs, convictions and aspirations. They see – miraculous survival in the modern world – a townscape in tune with their delicacy. They breathe a sigh of relief. They can breed in peace and pour forth their ratty soul-searching jigsaw perceptions into a vacuum of attentive, nodding, smiling yawns. Is anyone listening? Can they be spared from organized social-utilitarian genocide? Even rats, after all, have rights. And even if the population cannot be forced – even with the help of the most advanced and coercive medical technology, with drips, enemas and suppositories – to consume poetry, at least from time to time it can be flaunted in their faces. Poetry is not dead – it has just entered the terminal rodent stage.

From time to time, at regular intervals – or is it at prescribed times of the year, like the mating of lemmings? – the poets surge up from the sewers, the unknown pits where they lurk, and like those irritating little green flies that suddenly infest the air in the first hot days of spring pour into the open streets of the City. The City even permits them to organize their own nesting and mating ground in the Place St Sulpice, which is immediately converted into a labyrinth of wooden green stalls laid out around the fountain like a cerebral medieval fair. The Marché du Poésie gives heart to the despised practitioners of this dubious and ignoble craft. Dozens of open stalls lay out the verbal wares that otherwise would be impossible to find. Bearded bards from the Andes sit behind volumes of their work printed on furry paper like illegal drug dealers waiting for the military police to arrive with wailing sirens. Silver-haired Dadaist Furies sit by small television screens showing the pantomime torture of armadillos and bastard dogs while behind them hang tattered flags with stirring slogans: DADA AVEC NOUS! . . . and in a corner of the labyrinth, right across from the police station on the rue de Mézières, a small stage with, for backdrop, a blown-up photo of a Viennese café plays host to performing poets who sing unaccompanied with plaintive, sentimental, mock-furious voice into a microphone before an audience whose faces betray not the slightest hilarity, irony or amazement. Incredible liberty! Extraordinary cultivation and high-mindedness! Who has not noticed, however, that the principal emotion now delivered by the formidable emotion-guns of Poetry – and it is only when they sing live on stage that you are aware of the fact – is an acute and febrile embarrassment? What is the meaning of this emergence of embarrassment as the principal response to this rigorous and superbly pedigreed emotion-discharging activity? Try as you may to control the blushes that cross your face as you listen, skilfully as you may discipline the hilarious rolling of your intestines as they laugh instead of your lips, you cannot deny the truth to yourself as soon as you are alone: you are filled with a terrible and lugubrious embarrassment. You are filled with the same anguish you might feel witnessing the mental breakdown of your favourite aunt as she confessed her most intimate and shameful sexual deviations in front of a large audience in a public park. You do not know where to turn. The emotions come reeling out left and right, anger against the killing of whales, anger against menstruation, anger against the startling increase in the number of home videos, indignation against frivolity and starvation, nuclear chess games and the Bosses. This, in fact, would be acceptable if it were not for the sudden and unpredictable flashes of utterly immoral lyricism. Lyricism is a code; it has its own Morse syllables that come out in wooden and histrionic combinations. It makes your flesh crawl. You can sense the combinations coming before they come. The onset of the lyrical – which now is always self-consciously tamed with knowing and nauseous intellectualisms – makes your viscera flap in the convulsion of an internal snigger. The men are in crisp white shirts and ponytails like off-duty bullfighters; the women are greyish and have little fists which they hold out in front of their eyes as they whine.

Everywhere in the labyrinth of poetry there are Noble Sentiments scribbled over the walls with paint brushes in an attempt to recreate the atmosphere of anarchist spontaneity. In the cage of your dreams I am unchained. Vote for the dictatorship of dreams! Displacement is our idyll. The jungle is filled with yellow eyes. It is always dreams, freedom, humanity, aspiration, harmony, regret. By the UNESCO stall: 'It is the function of poets to dream of peace; it is the function of politicans to undo their dreams.' Everywhere you look there is the self-righteous imagery of doves, lovely girlish faces, olive branches, astrological signs. You can browse through the collected works of obscure labourers of the word whom you imagine – in a moment of depressing clairvoyance – sitting in troglodytic caves under bare light bulbs encrusted with incinerated flies pouring out their black hearts on to pieces of toilet paper which they send to their publishers rolled up inside good-luck charms. 'Gomorrah and Dusseldorf', 'The Analytic Syringe', 'Aids Sonnets Part 7 Interlude', 'Black Spaces no. 4', 'The Songs of Demented Bees', 'Haikus from Kurdistan', 'Bare Zones, Night,' 'Helices', 'Spirogyras and Charms', 'Chrysopolis 47' . . . the whorl of titles is eclipsed only by the possibility that the mournful vitamin-deficient faces behind the displays are the authors themselves, sporting as they do a well-earned but demeaning eccentricity. Oh yes, they are against the order of things. It is their divine task to be a thorn in the side of power, to spit in the face of science and give voice to the abused multitudes of dolphins. You know what they are against: you would never see them having a coffee with a capitalist, a captain of industry or an officer of the World Bank. No, they live in the superior world of superior moral perceptions, from which vertiginous height they look down on the pathetic mess of the existing world order.

In another corner of the compound youthful painters hurl brushes at a cardboard wall, there is a sound of guitars in the air and the sky grows hotter and more colourless. The massive façade of the church leers over the pretenders to the throne of the *ars poetica*, the dark bearded faces, barely hiding their highly civilized dreams filled with falling stars, jaguars and *compañero* hymns, twitch with uncertainty in the face of so much metropolitan sympathy. The compressed heads of the radical poets begin to look smaller and smaller, denser and denser, more and more closed in upon themselves. And the peasant-poetaster – who is naturally in their midst – suddenly feels cold, he would like to escape, and as the feeling of claustrophobia increases he begins to look for a way out of the Marché du Poésie, which is as insane as Minos's original maze. The reveries of freedom and the dithryambs of ecstasy are beginning to ferment unpleasantly in his bowels and if he doesn't find a toilet soon . . . but just as he is about to flee the encampment of professional madmen in the Place St Sulpice dressed up in their corduroy trousers and embroidered blouses, he catches sight of an acquaintance, a long-standing acquaintance in fact, staggering quite drunk by the fountain in the middle of a group of Young Communists who are cheering him on as he declaims some absurd rhymes in honour of President Ortega. With a sigh of relief, he recognized this ugly bear of a man as Salvador Flamingo Ortiz, the great exiled political bard of Guatemala whose elegies in honour of deceased liberators have earned him a bitter lifelong banishment in the suburb of Ivry-sur-Seine, where the local ruling Communist Party have awarded him a meagre stipend and a flat on the rue Marat. What an unexpected collision! They embrace and the Guatemalan's foul breath strikes the peasant's face with some force. In truth, the Hero of the Latin-Proletarian Word is a little depressed. Life out in the red suburbs is beginning to get to him. He can't write poetry any more. The life of an exile has lost its glamour and besides there are thousands of them now, Latin Americans of all descriptions spouting their committed extravaganzas in the deep of the night, all of them hanging on to the hem of the Paris robe with their teeth and gulping down the poisoned fruit of lionization followed by utter obscurity.

'They put me on the radio,' Flamingo laments heavily, wiping his lips. 'They make me read my poems and they're in Spanish, you see, no one understands a word. What do they care about the revolution brother, what do they know about . . . our fatality, our boredom, our Procastres beds, our death worship, our Iberian backwardness, our Arab sensibilities, our loquacious incubi, our love of cruelty, our self-pity, our Yankee-exploited raw materials, our *grandeur raté*, our superiority complex and our inferiority complex, our non–European Europeanism, our magnificent love of words, our purple rhetoric, our tangos, our exotic birds, our amazing vitality, our auto-criticism, our flaming spirituality, our heresies, our maritime blood, our leprosy, our sublime baroque architecture, our . . .'

It is difficult to stop him. They are caught up in a whirlwind of words, Flamingo red in the face, rotating his arms like a windmill with all his Quixotian charlatanism blazing in his eyes, and before long they are rolling together out of the square, the Guatemalan pulling large bugs out of his greying frizzled beard and miniature bottles of cooking brandy out of his numerous stench-filled pockets which are attached to a kind of flowing quiltwork coat. They fly through the streets while Flamingo pulls out one two-inch bottle after another, presses it to his lips and with one heroic suck empties the contents. The streets are gold and aquamarine. A tramp walks by with an enormous book under his arm entitled *A Short Course in Miracles*. The gridwork of alleys tilts in space with the bravura of the half-broken lance of our famous Castilian knight and the fat Mesoamerican whose eyes are slanted like the obsidian felines of his ancestors bawls and burps his way through his compositions, which complement in their hysterical way the alarming tendency of the metropolis to fall away continually from under their feet.

'There's a man . . . Fidel! I'd lick frankincense from his feet. Oh, you don't understand. You come from the hinterland of fog and greasy chocolates. We're omni-copulators. We dance with the cosmic samba while you . . . you sit behind your computers and get irradiated! We should have cut your hearts out right at the beginning. Ah, little girl in Cartagena. Little thighs opened up . . . like an artichoke heart. And Monica in Porto Cruz, blue like a Portuguese tile, glazed and miniaturized . . . as small as I like them. I'm getting horny just thinking about them, the Austral virgins. *Muchachas en la liga!* I have them all laid out, in my head, artichoke hearts and all. And Fidel too. Yes, you may sit behind a computer, gringo-heads, but you will never know the moronic ecstasies of screwing tiny Monica Artichokeheart Lipatti on the balcony of her father's banana plantation while butterflies drifted through the air to a sound of drowning mermaids far out in the bay of Porto Cruz . . . you will never refind El Dorado!'

The City of Poets and Exiles is stuck like a band of coloured cardboard to the inside of Flamingo Ortiz's and our peasant's brains, which does not however prevent them from soon taking to the air and flying above it with all the agility of aerial beings in a baroque play. As the moon rises they head south-east, flying over the dome of the Panthéon and the minaret of the Mosque, over the Austerlitz station and down to the glass and concrete towers of Chinatown, the Guatemalan still reciting his jungle hymns in a guttural bass voice and exhorting the peasant to magnificent acts of revolutionary heroism. Within a few minutes they are at the Porte d'Ivry and there is a change in the air. The Guatemalan, for all his complaints, feels immediately at home and condescends to return to *terra firma*. They are on radical soil once more. Flamingo expands his lungs and breathes in the sweet air of liberty. They are in the Commune of Ivry, the Communist suburb sandwiched between the appropriately named Le Kremlin-Bicêtre and the industrial section of the Seine lined by the N.4 as it leaves the City in the direction of the Marne, a town which is twinned with Section 9 of the socialist metropolis of Prague. Here the realities of international solidarity have overcome national chauvinisms. The horizonal world of the suburbs announces the end of the monumental City and the beginning of a barbarized, diluted sub-City, an outer periphery of incompletion and imperfection. The forms of the City are here flattened out at the edges. Brick replaces carved masonry. An alternative empire of taste is in force. The looming factories, warehouses, industrial installations and swathes of grimy houses sit uncomfortably but immovably under a film of dust. The river moves gloomily between them, unsure of where to go. The skyline, seen only from the overhead motorways that skirt and cross it, is a crazy scramble of pylons, towers and belching chimneys. The snaking glow-worm trains that slide across it at night illumine only miles of low walls, construction sites and empty playing fields. Visigothic monuments erupt from time to time out of the flat planes of this endless, semi-developed horizon, pinpoints of arrogant reflection from which sinking suns sometimes bounce back their tired rays. The net of lights spread over it is thin. Logic and dominating reason have been seduced by the attractions of low-density chaos. The outlying towns are meshed together violently, they sleep in obscurity, keeping their visual horrors coquettishly to themselves. From the centre of the City, you cannot even hear their breathing.

Then why does the Guatemalan feel so at home in Ivry-sur-Seine? Because he is filled with the knowing resentment of the exile. You think you know the real Paris – Eiffel Tower, Champs-Elysées, frilly knickers? This is the real Paris! The Paris of proletarian decency and toil, streaking concrete and whirls of dust. Bobigny, Ivry, Aubervilliers, Malakoff . . . the man who hates centres of any kind, who has been brought up as a peripheral, has an instinctive sympathy for these underbellies of the haughty City. Flamingo rolls his eyes miserably and prepares for a bout of self-pity. His lips are tired. We are in the suburbs. It's no use pretending here – no one is listening. All we can do is take our consolation from the great murals splashed over the suburb's walls depicting, in the otherwise deceased style of Diego Rivera, the class struggles in Nicaragua and El Salvador. We have left the City. We have left the contemporary age. We are once more in the unstable and dislocating hinterland of fantasy.

Prague 9

✤

One day long ago, almost at the limits of living memory, the inhabitants of Ivry-sur-Seine woke up to find that they were no longer a part of the Greater Paris area, that they were no longer in fact a part of France at all. By some miraculous administrative sleight of the hand the entire town had been ceded to the government of the People's Republic of Czechoslovakia, and more precisely to Section 9 of Prague. With what joy and gratitude did the citizens greet this astonishing transition from capitalism to socialism! They danced for days in the streets. And who can say that the rest of Paris does not look at them with envy and respect? Who can deny that Prague 9 is one of the most desirable residential suburbs in Europe, complete with clean streets, wholesome schools and giant socialist hypermarkets? If the Communist Party of Ivry has held on to its exalted office of official puppet ever since through intimidation, manipulation and large-scale electoral fraud, who can deny that this continuing maintenance of transnational dictatorship has been accepted by a docile and contented population with the greatest of political enthusiasm? At times they even forget the ring of mental barbed wire that separates them from the City. They have even begun to dream in Czech.

The symbol of this momentous transition to a normally superior mode of production is the Carrefour shopping centre. Only when the weary citizens entered the wide boulevards of the food department stuffed with millions of tons of fresh and tinned produce, ringed with vast *charcuterie* and cheese counters and equipped even with a motor accessories' aisle did they realize that they were finally part of the Marxist-Leninist world. Never before had they seen such dizzying arrays of commodities sitting so effortlessly and naturally on so many unmobbed shelves! At last they could enjoy what every street cleaner and sewage sweep in Prague had enjoyed for decades. The propaganda of the capitalist media fell away from their eyes and they went back to their theoretical texts with a renewed vigour and conviction. For in the carefully structured world of Prague 9 no one wants for anything and food queues are a quaint nightmare of the past.

The town itself has been built as a logical continuation of this social felicity. At its centre stands the crenellated Centre Commercial designed ironically to echo the Crown of Thorns. Originally intended, no doubt, as an all-encompassing pseudo-organic architectural sponge capable of fulfilling all the community's needs with the minimum of useless effort, it has grown old with the grace of a terminal cancer that cannot quite get the upper hand over its victim. The clustered thorns of this colourless sea urchin of bleached concrete thrust upward through plots of trees, intersecting ramps, spiral stairwells and globular sci-fi lamps planted in a paroxysm of 1960s optimism. A mixture of private residences and shopping malls, the Centre carefully cultivates a druidical atmosphere: at its centre, at the deepest level of the complex, surrounded by an insane whorl of Cubist stairs and vertiginous planes, stands a huge chestnut tree flanked on all sides by spooky funnels, denticulated roofs and abstract windows – evidently the last remains of a disappeared age too awkward to uproot. This dry well of stone with the trunk at its bottom is still and dark. The pale grey steel banisters that mark the descent to its base are a deliberate sneer in its face. In fact the playful horror of this integrated environment, this tittering version of the neo-Stalinist future gone wrong, presents the future as an impressive lugubrious self-parody. There are faces in the windows! There are people sauntering in the brutal interior arcades with their Czechoslovakian shop windows! Ramps, escalators, grottoes covered with graffiti, bleeding concrete, horrible pale mauve and orange ceiling panels entirely of the period, a whole grammar of ugliness elaborated with breathtaking confidence and wit. It has been designed as a terrifying maze which only those armed with coloured threads will succeed in safely navigating. We are truly in Prague, city of labyrinths, absurd trails and lost beings. And Section 9 is the showcase of the city!

Across the street the dutiful tourist may view, if he lounges awhile on one of the Centre's amiable and leisurely Spartan balconies (those terraces and projections that tumble down the sides of the edifice like tea plantations cut into the side of a tropical mountain), the artful realization of a full-scale de Chirico nightmare. An ochre and white mound of interlocking blocks assembled in order to remind the cockroaches of their subdued destinies. To his left, at the other end of the high street, is the Place de la République with its confused sculptures in liver-red stone and fountains of foamy green water set among zigzagging pebble stairs. In the whirlpools of traffic its delightful subtleties go entirely unnoticed. From here, however, the traveller to Section 9 can take the rue Marat, which leads back into the lazy maze of provincial tree-lined streets with small brick houses, villas and clumps of apartment blocks as far as the rustic Place Parmentier. A statue of Marianne stands in the gravel dust-bowl in her arcane republican headgear and fascia. Billboards pinned to walled-up shop fronts bearing the indefatigable image of Philippe Herzog, Communist deputy and anti-Yankee hero, surround her. It is a typical Marcel Carné suburb, lacking only the multitudes of bicycles of *Le Jour se lève*. On one side of the square is the A la Boule d'Ivry café, whose clouded interior will reveal, on cold winter nights, stoned Turkish faces assembled like illumined pumpkins around the tables. Above the café, printed African fabrics hang on the window clothes lines. The slope between the rues Marat and Robespierre is covered with the model habitations of happy and faithful workers and their broods of contented Communist Youth. The walls are plastered with demands from the said Youth ('Assez de bla-bla: Prix Nobel pour Mandela!'), while the embankments on the rue Robespierre are covered with demotic scenes of sugar harvests inscribed around the brazen logo VIVA NICARAGUA. By the giddy brown brick apartment blocks separated by verdant spaces, the Espace Vert Marat houses a dazed tramp sitting on a rock. The park and houses are so quiet the sound of birds can be heard. It is only lower down, among the old nineteenth-century factories converted into loft space, that the trains can also be heard slicing through the streets, parks and brick compounds. It is a shame only that they are not equipped with sirens and hellish bells. The administrators of Prague 9 have carefully made their trains anonymous. One wonders merely if the doors are locked by the police as they pass through . . .

Continuing his aimless and peaceful walk, the impressed tourist might also run into one of the municipality's demagogic festivals. He might, for example, catch the annual cycle race that runs its course through the town centre and which is supervised with true revolutionary fervour by squads of heavy 'officers' incessantly blowing into shrill little whistles. The judges' stand is set up by the town hall. Under a red, white and blue canopy fat men in tricolour breeches sit with tight red Phrygian caps perched on their heads. Everyone blows whistles, there are literally dozens of these buzzing 'officers' ordering people around, screaming and whistling at every car that passes by. The citizens of Prague 9 stand around on the pavements and observe the young cyclists flying past with odd murmurs and winks. The vitality of the beloved Party and its visionary policies can be read in every attendant face. He has seen these same faces before, stomping down the Boulevard Raspail on a summer afternoon with the same ludicrous hats, charging after bourgeois girls along the pavements on either side of a demonstration and behaving in the way that red-blooded eternally erect proles should. Oh, how we love the people, the tricksy, tipsy, fun-loving, naughty, brawny, golden-hearted salts of the earth! Let them chase after a bit of stuck-up pussy while marching in the *quartiers* where they don't belong, it serves the middle classes right. Vengeful moronic, Dryopithecus-style atavisms? Wash your mouth out with soap! André Olivier and Joelle Crépet, guardians of Action Directe, will come looking for you with a pair of shears to cut out your tongue! In the year of the bicentennial of 1789, in addition, the City is drowning in tides of indifference and it is therefore necessary to bring people to their senses, back to reality, to the principle of the guillotine. Faced with the imminent death of politics, the nabobs of Ivry, of Bobigny, of Aubervilliers, are forced to throw stones in all directions in order to resuscitate the masses' taste for dialectics, the colours red, white and blue and flashy effusions of passionate, numbing rhetoric with all the rich substance and mental spice of mustard gas.

On the Pacific-FM radio station, the sinister-looking Herzog, who suffers from an unfortunate resemblance to an SS executioner, declares his solidarity with that great martyr for Latin

American freedom, Manuel Noriega. The logic is inescapable: since the evil Yankees are trading in dead infants' internal organs all over the continent, it is only right that any resistance to them should be openly supported. Meanwhile, at Père Lachaise, the Communist faithful from many countries, including the rest of Czechoslovakia, gather around the Party's new memorial for the partisans of the FTP-MOI killed for the Cause, while Georges 'Iron Man' Marchais reads a few lines from Aragon, which are followed by more of the red bard's work read by other Party faithfuls along with the last letters of Guido Brancadoro. A choir sings the Chants des Partisans echoed by the Carmagnole battalion, while L'Harmonie de la RATP intones the Internationale and the Marseillaise. Everything is correctly in place, the noble words, the mosaics of Verdiano Marzi representing the Dove of Peace so beloved of the Stalinists of the 1940s, the political nostalgia for that golden decade of glory and power. Only, a ghost is present . . . the phantom of *perestroika*. The evil spirt of consumerism has prised the people away from doves, olive branches and red flags. As the tide of history goes out, small puddles, sandy pools and pockets of slime are left forlornly behind to continue the tradition, but there is still a hankering for history's ocean, for its communal depths and waves.

In the depths of his wretched little apartment on the rue Marat Flamingo Ortiz raises his heart in defiance of the inevitable, the shocking imminence of oblivion. It is not that history is going to conflict with the development of the two-millennium Plan but that it is going to pass it by rudely without raising an eyebrow. He is filled with despair. But at least he has the creature comforts of the Carrefour which only citizenship of Prague Section 9 could ever have conferred upon him. Outside his window he dreams of choirs of revolutionary maidens singing 'Les Temps des Cérises' over a background of gunfire. He imagines global convulsions and economic reversions. He becomes weepy at the thought of manual toil. Ortiz, Ortiz, flaming pink flamingo of the suburbs, your time is nearly up and your hair needs a cut. You are about to be turned into strawberry jam. Your songs are about to be turned into TV dog food commercials. I am romantically attached to your kind, the peasant ruminates, to your civilized bookishness and high ideals, but we must nevertheless recognize that you once hung a picture of Stalin from the walls of Nanterre and that you have never smelt the shit on your own hands. You have what I might call selective nostrils. You are the stale breath of the past though not yet the fetid stench of the future (you are at least to be admired for that). Looking around your study so cosily lodged in the backstreets of Prague 9 I feel a light and refreshing urge to vomit in your face. Who knows how terrifying you were when you were young, and how gruesomely crude and star-struck. You admire yourself for your ever-renewable ideals, for your capacity to remain always, deep down, the same man, the same little runt who once raved about the abolition of money and the giving of all power to the Soviets. But I have to tell you, dear friend, fellow conspirator and cultured appreciator of our mutual addictions, you are a shit-bag underneath everything, your breath stinks with your nauseously eternal 'youthfulness' and – more than anything else, I must confess – I would dearly love to sodomize you with a glowing poker. I have only one thing I wish to say to you as you sit here under your plaster busts of Manuel de Falla and Gramsci, and that in the sweet tones of friendship: go pop your revolution, and as you lie dying of the clap which the old bitch will doubtless give you, I will stuff roses up your backside and sing you songs from the Pampas with the aid of a Monoprix harmonica. Everything inside your head is nothing more than a brief history of murder. And though murder is undoubtedly an almost infinite subject, the history that you have neatly stored in your frontal lobes could be written, with an effort at elegance, on the back side of a postage stamp. It is the end, comrade. In the brief but universal history of murder we are nothing more than minor criminals executed on a winter morning no one knows where and buried under a municipal car park. There is only time for the dreams that pass in harmony with underground beetles through the craniums of peaceful corpses; for no dreambook, however humbly it may have been written in a single miserable head, can fail to have a valedictory epilogue filled with fireworks and petty deliriums. We can dream at last of all the murders we would have liked to have committed had fate bent our way . . .

A Brief History
of Murder

As he grows older, ever more conscious of his thirty years, the peasant becomes increasingly obsessed with death. Lurid misgivings fill his days, while his nights are given over to dreams about the City's most famous dealers of death. He therefore finds himself, for example, in the suave presence of Thierry Paulin, the dashing Caribbean murderer of thirteen old ladies subsequently cut down by Aids in the Fresnes prison hospital. In front of his eyes the mass killer bursts into tears in one of his neurotic fits, then turns on a warm and handsome smile. In other dreams he runs into François Bertrand, the nineteenth-century necrophile soldier who disinterred bodies in the Montparnasse cemetery, or the smart black knights of the Gestapo. He is aware of the presence of coffins all around him, the alternative necropolitan cities that underlie the punily tiny city of the living. If he is awake at night he does not fail to peruse through long hours his favourite book: Pierre Mariel's *Guide occulte et pittoresque des cimetières*, through which he can ponder the fate of Egyptian mummies accidentally buried under the Place de la Bastille and the mysterious destiny of the ancient Jewish cemetery of the rue de Flandre. The City has swallowed its own dead and hidden their traces. The history of murder which he is so longing to write throws up its clues with a sly and disgraceful humour. The City's violence covers itself with silence. In 1867, during the construction of the Boulevard Arago, workers discovered, near the *impasse* Longue-Avoine, a human skeleton and that of a dog, the head lying six metres from the body. There was no exit from the enclosed gallery. A guillotine once stood at the near-by Place St Jacques. And decapitated heads have been found all over the City, they are by no means uncommon. Executed corpses are piled high in the City's foundations, heads without names or dates, a cruel sediment of history's losers and its most gifted killers. He loves the catacombs, with their street names and mock squares, the Rotonde des Tibias, 300 kilometres and six million dead. How much he regrets the passing of the communal ditches of Les Halles, whose smell suffused the heart of the City! How much he would like to discover the origins of the hundreds of cat skulls found in a wall near the Odéon! At the back of his mind he is ever mindful of the vanished occupants of the Zone, the strip of *bidonvilles* constructed after 1941 along the line of the former fortifications almost as a living City of the Dead, the Jewish children in the concentration camp at Beaune-la-Rolande, the rifle range at the wartime Air Ministry on the Boulevard Victor where the hand prints of the executed are burned into the wall. Everywhere he turns, this macabre sub-history winks at him from under shadows and stones. He has lain on his bed during a hot summer and listened to the distant detonations of terrorist bombs popping around the City. He has watched from the safety of his skull Lebanese hit-men rolling down the rue de Rennes, tumbling grenades into jean shops. Borne along on obscure tidal waves of hatred, the dispossessed, those who feel cheated of paradise, run through the alleys and fetid back streets gun in hand, ready like Essex, the would-be Black Panther, to pump a few white pigs full of Bulgarian bullets. He sees the ghost of Marie Antoinette urinating in the courtyard of the Conciergerie before her execution tumbril, the head of the Princesse de Lamballe bobbing up and down on a spike and the heart of Bertier de Sauvigny ripped out of his body and hurled at the Hotel de Ville before his head was hacked off by the mob.

The City breeds its own convulsions of savagery. The Massacre of the Innocents is replayed a century later in the assassinations of the Commune. The City has spawned Stalin and Mussolini, it gave birth to systematic murder as theatre and the butcher instinct of the progressive modern state. Murder is mechanized by the guillotine and the citizen integrated into the hunting pack. The City which invented modern political murder has seen its own nightmares realized and then forgotten. The 20,000 slaughtered during the Commune are buried hastily under the very pavements where shoppers and bickering lovers amble today, their mouths upturned, their bones sinking continually downwards. The ditches of Belleville are filled with remains erased from memory. The empire of murder has turned the City into its most glorious satrapy and relegated it to the status of civilized province. Murder has moved elsewhere and a local quiet has fallen over the streets interrupted only occasionally by the splutter of amateur killers' weapons in the middle of the red nights of the age of radical chic. And the curious thing is that the peasant is nostalgic for the lost golden age of murder, he correctly identifies it as the City's greatest period of vitality and influence . . . the history of murder is not just the history of murder. The murdered have come to outnumber the murderers and the killing is now principally left to psychopaths and foreigners. Murder has beaten a retreat, and the stillness it has left behind is both frustrating and unnerving. Sitting uneasily in his humble rooms at no. 37 rue André Antoine, he keeps one ear perpetually alert in readiness for the next incursion of murder into its happy grounds. But there is nothing but peaceful turbulence. There is nothing but the immobility of discreetly forgotten mass graves. The City has other things on its mind.

We would like to educate you with some parables concerning the nature of evil, greed and time using a few timeless gems of wisdom from Kazakhstani folktales and Guahibe proverbs, but we know that, like our cynical hero, you will only nod your head and continue taking your *café crème* as you always do, brainwashed to the bottom of your soul by the comfortable disguises of the City of Capital. No doubt you think that there is nothing to be done about it. But the peasant, suspiciously peering into the faces of his co-tenants, the meat-man upstairs whose figures of speech are full of homicide, Aladdin downstairs whose marbled eyes are strangely wild after an evening on the weed, the Khomeinist from the top floor whom he sometimes surprises creeping furtively down the stairs with volumes of Mohammed Sayed Qutb and Hassan al-Bannah under his arm, is nevertheless unable to sleep peacefully: he is a haunted man, haunted by his sudden and precipitous loss of youth and the violence that seems to be brooding under the City's skin.

Sometimes also he accidentally stumbles across little notes written in blue crayon which the Yugoslavian leaves provocatively on the stairs, garbled quotations from Qom clerics, menacing gobs of hate from the Master of Tehran. 'Every part of the body of a

203

non-Muslim is impure, even the hair on his hand and his body, his nails, and all the various secretions of his body . . . This is why Islam has put so many people to death: to safeguard the interests of the Muslim community. Islam has obliterated many tribes . . .' To which the neo-fascist, in similar militant vein, lets drop cryptic messages of his own deliberately penned in green crayon (green, he has remembered, was the anti-revolutionary colour during the Terror, but he has forgotten that it is also the colour of Islam). 'The only tribes about to be obliterated here are the turban-wearing sort . . . long live Charles the Hammer!' The *concierge* himself, probably anxious to preserve peace and harmony in the war of crayon notes, leaves scrubby notes pinned to the banisters by the vestibule written in crazy letters that dance across the paper: 'Smile, friends – Venus is horny tonight!' Madame Pompom leaves nothing at all unless it is the occasional demand to eradicate all traces of extra-departmental cooking from the stairway and elaborate signs ordering passers by to observe a strict code of deferential silence in front of her door. And the girl on the ground floor is content merely to put round green stickers on the rectangular panes of glass in the hall door bearing strident Green slogans: 'CFCs – *Nein Danke*!' 'Kill the hamburger!' 'Save the atmosphere – become a druid today!'

In this way the various occupants of no. 37 discourse with each other as their place of abode, along with the planet so precariously attached to it, spins through space in a vague ellipse, carrying with it a strange odour of lemon grass and cardamom pods, and only the peasant who sits secluded in his room overlooking the chestnut trees of St Jean refuses to communicate with them in this way, preoccupied as he is with the history of murder and the recent appearance of blue comets in the section of sky between the constellations of Cassiopeia and Auriga. The dreambook he has so clumsily composed has only one chapter left, and that can only be concerned with what he thinks he will do when he dies, when he will be free at last to write the masterpiece he has always dreamed of writing. He has no need to fall asleep as he composes this last and most revealing chapter, any more than he has needed the inducements of sleep during his various pilgrimages around the City of his cretinous but valuable dreams. He has only to sit still and permit his latent anguish and despair at the progress being made all around him by the sneering power of time to surface and break into a huge, purple mental sore which has become the companion of his nights and which pours its pus constantly into his sleeping brain. He is kept alertly asleep by the action of poison. He is going to die on a night filled with blue unnamed comets passing obliquely through the Milky Way and the dreambook will receive its finalizing signature. There will be nothing left but a white room filled with imaginary manuscripts, a glass of water on a table and a beautiful peacock quill with a gold nib. The dreambook will finish by falling asleep itself. The constellations will polka crazily across unaccustomed parts of the sky and as some quirky supernatural cock begins to crow he will pick up the gold quill and begin to write . . .

Coda

We see, he sees, glimpses of rain-soaked boulevards, stunted and spiked trees in triumphal mourning, women in boleros and bavolets, crinolines and tarlatan, sloe-eye tarts in laced boots maudlin in front of suicidal absinthes, spires and domes, distant vistas frozen in the sly tones of ash, moonlit parks hidden behind railings upon which the bodies of adolescents can sometimes be seen impaled, vast arteries ribbed with lamps, the slow cooing of the trees, the music of funeral hearses and barrel-organs stacked with sentimental prison songs . . . Paris performing its St Vitus's dance of cliché, in the throes of its self-induced carnival of dreams.

Fragments of celluloid help him: Arletty dancing through leafy slums, Pépé le Moko dreaming of home, the thief in René Clair's *Le Millionaire* escaping from a hotel to infuriated cries from the propretior rising in a crescendo of accusation: 'Con-man! Thief! Fraud! Bastard!' thoroughly exasperated . . . 'Artist!' A slim crooner with wild pop-out eyes, is it Charles Trenet?, ambles foward to a microphone:

> Cleopatra was a tantalizer,
> She did it with her atomizer.

The exploded city will revolve in a shaft of light in his head like a neolithic arrow-head displayed in a damp provincial museum.

It is already disappearing over the centuries with a noise like an army of African ants . . . Babylonian confusion . . . awakening hatred of the present . . . twittering, self-inflicted crisis . . . lust for apocalypse . . . lust for totem poles . . . lust for deserts and Aztec masks. The noise of the ant-city rolls away down the centuries while he sits in his celestial cubicle, and its smoking domes, piles of refuse and recreational parks roll with it, spreading as far as the eye can see. His beloved metropolis spins like a coin on its allotted piece of earth and tumbles away into the dark edges of the world visible from his eternal window. Golden stone, noble façades, edifices of faith. Behind it buried in alluvial sand lie a stub of an iron tower, bales of paper tied with splendid pink ribbons, curious fragments of missiles, sculpted heads and glass pyramids browned by exposure to the atmosphere.

The peasant yawns and looks around his chamber filled with colossal manuscripts. Flies are crawling over the pages of his book. How did they get into Heaven? Why is it that he can still hear a siren wailing over the roof tops? He scratches his head and shrugs. Turning over on to his side, closing his eyes with the irony of those who have little interest in the rhythms of dreaming and waking, he falls asleep for five hundred and twenty eight years, six months, fourteen days, seven hours, thirty two minutes and eight seconds. He has hardly batted an eye-lid, but when he wakes the City has vanished into thin air.